BLUE BOOK 60 is published in the United States
by X60 MEDIA, LLC

Created by Billy Martin and Tim Malloy

For Officiating / Umpire resources visit: **ref60.com**

Necessary corrections and subsequent updates can be found at:

bluebook60.com

First Printing: June 2009 --- 11th Printing: January 2019

For bulk order requests please email:

info@ref60.com

FORWARD

Welcome to the all-new tenth release of *"Blue Book 60" – 2019 Fastpitch Softball Edition.* Our goal is to provide a comprehensive guide for fans, athletes, coaches and umpires that covers the most popular fastpitch rule sets from scholastic, to collegiate and even through USA international or popular travel softball competitions.

This book has been an Amazon bestseller for the past ten years and is updated every season with the latest rule changes for NCAA, NFHS, USSSA and USA Softball.

We are proud to say, 100 percent of the proceeds from this book are used for continuing education of officials and coaches in 80+ countries worldwide.

We hope you enjoy reading *"Blue Book 60"* as much as we did creating it.

"Your knowledge of the rules is something
that always can be questioned. So know them!"

–Billy Martin, Co-Creator
Former Supervisor of Basketball Officials – IAABO Camden, NJ Board 34
NCAA Fastpitch Umpire for Eastern Collegiate Softball Umpires
Scholastic Fast Pitch Umpire for the NJSIAA and West NJ Chapter #5

"Rule competency breeds calmness and confidence in chaos."

-Tim Malloy, Co-Creator
Former College Basketball Official (CBOA) , Front Office Executive for Philadelphia 76ers,
Former Secretary/Independent Assignor and long standing member of
IAABO Camden, NJ Board 34

ABOUT THE AUTHORS

Billy **Martin** has over 38 years officiating / umpiring experience with basketball and fast-pitch softball in the Southern New Jersey area.

Currently he is an NCAA umpire for the Eastern Collegiate Softball Umpires Association (ECSU) as well as a scholastic umpire for West (NJ) Chapter 5. Billy was fortunate and honored to be chosen to work various NCAA Division II and III conference championships including NCAA regional tournament selections and a New Jersey State Championship final assignment.

In the business world, Billy has more than 30 years of sales and marketing experience, most recently with Salesforce (NYSE:CRM), the industry leader in Customer Relationship Management and marketing tools.

Billy holds a Master's Degree in Education (MEd) specializing in Sports Medicine and a Master's Degree in Business Administration (MBA) in Technology Management.

He is also the co-author of four Amazon best-selling basketball officiating guides called, "Beyond the Rules" (**gobeyondtherules.com**) and the "GameTracker Journal." Billy is also the co-founder of "60 Seconds on Officiating" a destination site for over 100,000 officials in 80 countries worldwide (**ref60.com**).

Billy resides in Wildwood, NJ and loves boating, fishing, and just about any activity that will leave sand between his toes.

Contact Billy Martin:
Email: billymartin@comcast.net
Twitter: @crmbilly
LinkedIn: in/crmbilly

ABOUT THE AUTHORS

Tim Malloy, between the ebb and flow of a chronic illness that required 32 surgeries, has pushed forward and carved a path of distinction in both the world of basketball and business.

As a 40+ year veteran referee of IAABO Board 34, Tim has worked numerous New Jersey state playoff games and climbed the ladder to the college ranks. Tim officiated as a member of CBOA where he earned Division II and III playoff assignments.

Off the court, Tim was a front office executive for the NBA World Champion Philadelphia 76ers in 1983 and served as the team's Assistant Group Sales Director and Public Relations Director for seven seasons. Tim later worked as a Sales and Promotions representative for Converse Inc., where he was a two-time Salesman-of-the Year award winner. He also holds a U.S. Patent for a golf training device that received a 4-star rating in Golf Magazine and is the co-author of the sports reference books, *"GameTracker Journal"* and *"Beyond the Rules"* for basketball.

Tim is a graduate of St. Joseph's University (PA) and resides in West Deptford, NJ with his wife Pattie, son Matt and daughter Mary Frances.

Contact Tim Malloy via email:
board34@comcast.net

CONTRIBUTORS

We would like to give special thanks to all those who have given support and editorial contribution to make this project successful and have shared their knowledge with officials worldwide. Your expertise is greatly appreciated.

Allison J. Munch is the current New Jersey State Interscholastic Athletic Association (NJSIAA) Rules Interpreter and former rules committee member of the NFHS. She also currently serves as the West Chapter #5 Cadet Supervisor. Allison has umpired all levels of softball including high school, NCAA Nationals, and the ASA Nationals for over 40 years. She has mentored hundreds of successful softball officials throughout New Jersey and the Delaware Valley.

Ed Sadowski was formerly the USSSA's Fastpitch Umpire in Chief for the state of New Jersey. An NCAA Umpire with post-season and national championship experience, he also works at the scholastic level for the New Jersey State Interscholastic Athletic Association (NJSIAA) in its southern region.

Michael A. Schiro, Ph.D. came to officiating after a 15 year career as an NCAA Division II softball coach at Bloomfield College. He is currently Head Clinician and NCAA Rules Interpreter, for the Eastern Collegiate Softball Umpires (ECSU). Beginning his umpiring career in 1999, Mike has worked numerous ASA fastpitch tournaments at the state and regional level. In addition he has worked 8 fastpitch National tournaments including both the Men's and Women's Major and two 18 and under gold events. He is a member of the ASA Indicator Fraternity and has received the ASA Region 2 UIC Award for outstanding ability and loyalty. At the collegiate level, Mike has worked postseason NCAA tournaments each year since 2006 umpiring at both the Division II and Division III levels. He has served as a regional UIC twice – once at the Division II level and once at Division III.

CONTRIBUTORS

Diane Reuter is the New Jersey State UIC, assigner for South Jersey and 2018 member of the USSSA National Rules Committee representing the Northeast Region. Diane has been involved with fast pitch softball in many capacities for over 25 years including umpiring for 18+ years for NFHS (West Chapter #5), USSSA, NSA, GSA, Pony and Little League. She has been honored to work multiple NJSIAA Southern New Jersey, Sectional and State finals as well as the USSSA World Series Semi-Finals and Finals.

Don Briscoe is first and foremost a Board Member of the Duluth (Georgia) Softball Umpires Association. He is on the NCAA umpire staff of the Mid-Eastern Athletic Conference and seven other collegiate conferences, and currently serves as the National Rules Coordinator and Georgia State UIC for the United States Specialty Sports Association (USSSA). Don has umpired for 30+ years and has umpired 16 National/World Series tournaments for USA Softball, NSA, ISA and USSSA. Additionally Don has served as Umpire-in-Chief for four USSSA World Series.

Special thanks to the ...

Providing scholarships for individuals
that desire to experience the joy
of sports officiating.

Visit: ProjectZebra.org
for more info.

REFERENCES

The **"BLUE BOOK 60"** series provides **OFFICIALS, UMPIRES, COACHES,** and **PLAYERS** a consolidated "<u>**UNOFFICIAL**</u>" reference guide that compares and contrasts the predominant rule governing bodies. Please refer directly to the official rule sets for each organization, as **"BLUE BOOK 60"** is intended to provide "60 second bites" of relevant content. **"BLUE BOOK 60"** is meant to complement the official publications, **NOT REPLACE** them.

USSSA

United States Specialty Sports Association

The USSSA is a volunteer sport's governing body, non-profit organization based in Kissimmee, Florida. USSSA governs 13 sports across the US, Puerto Rico, various US Military bases, and Canada and has a membership of over 3.2 million.

USSSA Online News and Resources – www.usssa.com
611 Line Drive, Kissimmee, FL 34744 | Telephone: (321) 697-3636

NFHS

National Federation of State High School Associations

The NFHS, from its offices in Indianapolis, Indiana, serves its 50 member state high school athletic/activity associations, plus the District of Columbia. The NFHS publishes playing rules in 16 sports for boys and girls reaching 18,500 high schools and over 11 million students involved in athletic and activity programs.

NFHS Publications Order Department – www.nfhs.org
P.O. Box 361246 | Indianapolis, IN 46236-5324 | Phone: (800) 776–3462

 Index can be found on page 105.

REFERENCES
(Continued)

USA Softball (Formerly ASA)

USA Softball (formerly ASA) is the National Governing Body (NGB) of Softball in the United States and a member of the United States Olympic Committee. Founded in 1933 as the Amateur Softball Association (ASA), USA Softball sanctions competition in every state through a network of 70 local associations and has grown from a few hundred teams in the early days to over 165,000 teams today, representing a membership of more than 2.02 million. USA Softball also annually registers over 25,000 umpires across the U.S.

USA Softball – www.usasoftball.com
2801 NE 50th Street | Oklahoma City, Oklahoma 73111 | Phone: (405) 424-5266

NCAA
The National Collegiate Athletic Association

The National Collegiate Athletic Association (NCAA) is a voluntary organization through which many of the nation's colleges and universities govern their athletics programs.

NCAA Publications Online – www.ncaapublications.com
P.O. Box 6222
Indianapolis, Indiana 46206-6222
Phone: (317) 917-6222

ADDITIONAL RESOURCES

60 Seconds on Officiating:	**ref60.com**
Blue Book 60 Website:	**bluebook60.com**
Beyond the Rules (Basketball):	**gobeyondtherules.com**
Officiating Scholarships:	**projectzebra.org**

Logos and trademarks are property of their respective owners.
All rule references are copyrighted by their respective governing bodies.

NFHS 2019 Major Rule Changes

NFHS

Designated Media Areas

The media shall be prohibited from being in live-ball area. The home team or game management may designate an area for the media in dead ball territory. It is no longer acceptable to designate any area in live-ball territory for media to occupy during the game. Game management is still free to designate a media area anywhere in dead-ball territory.

The change minimizes risk of participants and others involved in the game. Previously, a ball was declared dead if the media area was occupied but remained live if it was unoccupied. The possibility that an area is considered a dead-ball area only at certain times during a game could create an unfair advantage for one team.

Bat (and Adjustable Knob)

The knob may be molded, lathed, welded or adjustable, but must be permanently fastened. This clarifies that an adjustable knob is permissible, provided the knob is permanently fastened by the manufacturer.

This is in reference to the recently approved "adjustable knob device" that is permanently fastened to the bat by the manufacturer. A knob may be adjustable but must be permanently affixed while being used in the game.

Defensive Face Shields

Defensive players are permitted to wear a shield (protection) on their face/head while in the field but it must be constructed of a molded, rigid material that is clear and permits 100 percent (no tint) allowable light transmission. In an effort to promote risk minimization, tinted eye shields are prohibited for defensive face/head protection.

The intent of this change is to make these shields, if worn, consistent with shields on batting helmets (1-6-7) and catchers masks (1-7-1).

NFHS Rule References
1-1-7, 1-5-2a, 1-8-4

Index can be found on page 105.

Illegal Pitch Penalty

Language to address a change in the penalty for an illegal pitch was included. Previously all base runners were advanced one base as well as a ball being called on the batter.

The approved change removes the advancement of base runners. Considering that an illegal pitch is designed to hinder the batter, the Softball Rules Committee felt that only the batter should receive an advantage from the penalty.

Now, in the case of an illegal pitch, the batter is awarded a ball. The penalty that permitted base runners to be awarded one base without liability to be put out is removed. The new language creates more balance between offense and defense. The batter should receive the award rather than runners already on base.

Pitcher Simulates Taking a Signal (Point of Emphasis)

While on the pitcher's plate and prior to bringing her hands together, the pitcher must take or simulate taking a signal from the catcher. A signal may be taken from a coach either by hand signals, verbal call, or by looking up on a wristband with a playbook/playcard. The signal obtained from the coach can be taken while on the pitching plate or while standing behind the pitcher's plate prior to taking a position on the pitcher's plate.

By rule, the only requirement is that no matter where or from whom the actual signal is obtained, the **pitcher must take a position on the pitcher's plate** with the hands separated and simulate taking a signal from the catcher. Requiring the pitcher to take position on the pitching plate and simulating taking a signal from the catcher prior to bring her hands together allows the batter to prepare for the start of the pitch.

If the pitcher does not pause after stepping onto the pitcher's plate to simulate taking a signal from the catcher prior to bringing her hands together, an illegal pitch should be called.

NFHS Rule References

6-1-1 PENALTY, 6-1-2 Thru 4 PENALTY, 6-2-1 PENALTY, 6-2-7 PENALTY

Proper Sliding Technique (Point of Emphasis)

One of a coach's responsibilities is to help reduce risk and injury to players whenever possible. This includes teaching proper sliding techniques as well as educating players on executing a legal slide (Rule 2-52).

Ensuring that players utilize proper technique when sliding will help reduce the potential injuries seen when a slide is performed. Ensuring that the slide is performed legally will also reduce the risk to the defender when a tag is being applied to a player sliding into a base.

Head Coach Listed on Lineup Card (Point of Emphasis)

Although not a requirement by rule, it is considered a best practice that the head coach list his/her name on the lineup card submitted at the pre-game conference. By listing his/her name on the lineup card, it assists both the umpire and other team if communications dealing with the game are required.

2019 NFHS Major Editorial Changes

Appeal Play

2-65-2: Clarifies there can be no appeal of the play that occurred prior to the umpire awarding an intentional walk.

Start of Pitch / Motion

6-1-2a, b: Clarifies what motion constitutes the start of the pitch and when the step back of the non-pivot foot may be taken.

DP/Flex -- Appendix H

An Appendix regarding DP/FLEX rules was added for quick reference into the NFHS Rule Book for 2019. See the "DP/Flex" section of this BlueBook for a detailed overview of this rule option.

NFHS Rule References
2-65-2, 6-1-2a, Appendix H

USSSA 2019 Major Rule Changes

USSSA

Tinted Face Shields

If an eye shield is worn attached to the batting helmet, it must be constructed of a molded rigid material that is clear and permits 100 percent (no tint) allowable light transmission. A chinstrap is optional.

Tournament Director's Uniform Discretion

Tournament directors may, on an individual basis, permit a player to participate while wearing a different style uniform for religious reasons, inclement weather, etc.

Non-Approved Bat Defined

BAT, NON-APPROVED. A non-approved bat is a bat that does not bear the current USSSA 1.20 BPF "thumbprint" certification mark, or a bat that is listed on the USSSA Withdrawn/Non-Compliant Bat List. EXCEPTION: Wood bats per 2-10-D.

Scoring on Game Winning / Walk-Off Awards

On a game-ending out-of- the park home run, ground-rule double, or awarded bases for overthrows into dead ball territory or detached player equipment, all runs shall score as if the game were to continue. In these cases, the winning margin may be more than one run. EXCEPTION: it is not possible for the winning margin to exceed the RUN RULE limits imposed in 4-4.

Reclassifies Improper Use of FLEX Player

Placing the FLEX player into one of the batting positions for someone other than the DP's position is considered an **illegal player** penalized per Rule 5-7. Placing the FLEX player in one of the first 11 positions in the batting order for someone other than the DP is illegal The use of an illegal player is correctable. PENALTY: An illegal player violation results in the immediate ejection of the illegal player and the head coach.

USSSA Rule References
2.1, 2.8, 3-Bat/Non-Approved, 2.6, 4.4j, 4.7

 ## Starting Pitchers No Longer Must Face a Complete Batter

It is NO LONGER REQUIRED that the starting pitcher must face one complete batter. If the starting pitcher is replaced before the first opposing batter has been put out or advanced to first base, the pitcher may play or re-enter at another position, or return to pitch following proper substitution rules and regulations.

Illegal Pitch Penalty - Ball Awarded Only

An illegal pitch is a pitch that violates the pitching rule or is an effect for a rules violation. When an illegal pitch occurs, it shall be called immediately by the plate or base umpire. **EFFECT**: The pitch is declared a ball (only). Baserunners previously were awarded one base without liability to be put out. This penalty has been removed to be consistent with other codes and create more balance between offense and defense.

Entering Batter's Box with an Illegal Bat

The batter is called out when entering the batter's box with an illegal bat, or has completed their turn at bat using that bat and before the next pitch, legal or illegal -- **EFFECT**: The ball is dead immediately. On a batted ball, any runners not put out must return to the base occupied at the time of the pitch. Base runner advances on a non-contacted pitch are legal. The bat shall be removed from the team's possession. When the illegal bat is an altered or non-approved bat, the batter and head coach are also ejected.

2019 USSSA Major Editorial Changes

Rule 4 Sec 8 Clarifies runner responsibilities during a non-charged time-out. When a defensive player requests time to speak to one or more defensive players, base runners may not abandon the vicinity of their bases without It being a charged offensive conference. NOTE: If either team is charged with a conference, base runners are no longer restricted to the vicinity of their bases.

Rule 5 Sec 4 Clarifies when the FLEX may play offense-only. (See DP/Flex Section)

Rule 5 Sec 8 Clarifies when forfeiture applies for an ineligible player. The penalty for using an ineligible player is a forfeit of game in progress. For use of an ineligible player in a game previously completed, see Rule 13-5.

USSSA Rule References
4.5, 4.8, 5.4, 5.8, 6.3, 7.14, 8.14

 Rule 6 Sec 1 Clarifies when a pitcher has to "wipe off" her hands. The pitcher shall not at any time be allowed to use any moisture or foreign substance on the ball, the pitching hand or fingers nor do anything to deface the ball. A pitcher who licks their fingers must wipe the fingers off before bringing them in contact with the ball. Players are not permitted to deface the ball. No tacky or sticky substances are permitted.

Under the supervision and control of the Umpire, the following items may be used to dry the hand which is in contact with the ball: dirt (but not chalk), powdered resin and an approved drying agent.

Rule 6 Sec 1 Also clarifies that a pitcher may continue to warm up if the Umpire is still performing administrative duties. At the beginning of an inning five practice pitches (or throws) are permitted. Excessive warmup pitches (or throws) in excess of five shall be penalized. EXCEPTION: This does not apply if the umpire delays the start of play due to substitution, conference, injuries, or other umpire responsibilities. Reminder that a pitcher returning to pitch in the same half-inning shall not be allowed warm-up pitches.

Rule 8 Sec 3 Relocates responsibility of pitcher/catcher in bottom of first inning and clarifies consequence of declaring a sub unable to serve as a courtesy runner. If an eligible substitute is physically present but is unable to courtesy run because of injury or illness, that player shall be ineligible for the entire game if the team utilizes the LCAB courtesy runner option.

In the top of the first inning only, the pitcher and catcher are identified as those players listed as the pitcher and catcher; both must face at least the first batter on defense (one pitch). Thereafter, the pitcher and catcher are identified as the last players who physically played that position on defense. The pitcher or catcher must reach base legally by any means other than substitution in order to be eligible for a courtesy runner.

EXCEPTION: When an injury or disqualification occurs in the top of the first inning to the pitcher/catcher identified on the lineup card and she is unable to face the first batter in the bottom of the first inning, the player who ran for her is retroactively her substitute (unless the substitute was an LCAB courtesy runner), no longer a courtesy runner. All substitution rules apply, but the pitcher/catcher has left the game and may not return to the original pitching/catching position.

USSSA Rule References

6.1, 8.3

USA Softball 2019 Major Rule Changes

USAS

Organizational Logos

Remove restrictions from coaches, players and team representatives from displaying the names or logos of other softball associations on their uniforms. This rule change allows for other organizational logos to be on player and coaches uniforms.

Headwear Restrictions

Ball caps and visors are optional for players. If worn, they may be mixed and must be worn properly. Colors must be: black, white, gray, beige or team colors. The colors may be mixed and are not required to be the same for all team members. Handkerchiefs do not qualify as headwear and cannot be worn around the head or neck. Plastic visors are not allowed.

This change allows colors to be mixed when wearing caps or visors.

Numerals on Uniform

An Arabic whole number (0-99) of contrasting color, or outlined in contrasting color, at least three inches high, must be clearly visible on all uniform shirts.

This revises the requirement for the size and location of the number placed on the uniform jersey.

EP Listing in Batting Order

When batting up to all roster players, any additional batters shall be listed as an EP and may be listed anywhere in the batting order and may play defense at any position.

This change clarifies where EPs may be listed in the batting order for JO Fastpitch Pool Play.

USA Softball Rule References
3-6, 3-6A Effect 2, 3-6D, 4-1C, 5-3A

 ## Regulation Time Limit Games

All games played using a Time Limit will be considered Regulation Games regardless of the number of innings completed/played.

This change specifies that all games ending as a result of the Time Limit Rule will be considered Regulation Games.

Reporting Defensive Changes

Defensive changes involving the pitcher or catcher must be reported to the Plate Umpire to ensure the correct player may have a courtesy runner.

This change requires teams to report those defensive changes involving the pitcher or the catcher.

<u>USA Softball Rule References</u>
5-3A, 8-10A[4]

NCAA 2018-19 Major Rule Changes

NCAA **Runner's Lane**

The NCAA added several new rule references to the 30 foot area comprised of the last half distance between home plate and first base where the batter must run to avoid interfering with a fielder's attempt to receive a thrown ball. It is bounded by a 30-foot line drawn in foul territory parallel to and 3 feet from the first-base line, starting at a point halfway between home plate and the back edge of first base. If the infield is skinned, it is recommended the runner's lane be skinned.

The batter-runner **may not run outside the runner's lane and, in the umpire's judgment, interfere with the fielder** taking the throw at first base. Interference is ruled when either (foot of the batter- runner) is completely outside the runner's lane, in contact with the ground, and, in the judgment of the umpire, she interferes with the fielder taking the throw at first base.

Exceptions are as follows. She **may** run outside the runner's lane:
- If she has not yet reached the start of the runner's lane
- To avoid a fielder attempting to field a batted ball
- If she leaves the lane on her last stride in order to touch first base

The batter-runner is considered outside the runner's lane if either foot is completely outside either line and in contact with the ground.

EFFECT—The ball is dead, the batter-runner is out, and each base runner must return to the last base occupied at the time of the pitch. If the interference, in the umpire's judgment, is an obvious attempt to prevent a double play, the base runner closest to home plate shall also be called out.

Note: By again requiring the runner's lane to be drawn on the field this re-establishes the original intent of the rule, which is to create a protected area to run from home to first base and to prevent the runner from interfering with the defensive player receiving the ball and first base.

NCAA Rule References
2.28, 12.5.5, 12.17.1.5.2

Bats and Helmets

The **bat** barrel, taper and handle shall be of one piece or multi-piece permanently assembled. This rule updated deleted the words "two-piece interchangeable barrel construction" which is no longer relevant.

The bat shall have a knob of a minimum of ¼ inch protruding at a degree angle of 90 or less from the handle. It may be molded, lathed, welded or **adjustable** (newly added to the rule), but must be permanently fastened. A "flare" or "cone" grip attached to the bat will be considered altered. The knob may be taped or marked for identification as long as there is no violation of this section. The knob may be solid or hollowed out to house an embedded metric sensor.

If a **sensor** is used it shall:
- not affect performance
- be secured by a locking mechanism and a backup mechanism to keep it in place
- have a distinguishing "offline" mode to prevent data from being accessed during a game.

Note: Bats with adjustable knobs allow hitters to use one bat and have the benefit of adjusting the knob to different lengths to provide hand stability that a traditional knob provides, but do not provide any type of unfair advantage. The metric sensor allows for the increased advances in technology of bat construction and will offer hitters feedback on their swing after the game.

A defensive player may wear a **helmet**. If more than one player wears a helmet, the helmets must be the same color. Highly reflective, mirror-like chrome-finish helmets of any color are prohibited.

Note: Previously this was only for offensive players and now extends the same restrictions to the defense.

NCAA Rule References
3.3.1.1, 3.3.1.1.2, 3.3.1.7.2, 3.7.2 , 3.8.3.1

NCAA Field Maintenance

Maintenance of the field before and during games shall be the responsibility of the home-team management. The home team may **hand drag/rake the field** after a complete inning, provided it does not delay the start of the next inning. Additional in-game field maintenance may be requested by the umpire(s).

Umpire Reporting Time

The **umpires should report to the field** and notify the on-site administrator and home-team coaches of their arrival at least **one hour** before the start of the game.

Note: This standard procedure was changed from :45 minutes to one hour.

Cell Phone / Smartphone / Devices

Team personnel, including players, are prohibited from wearing any device capable of transmitting information while on the field (e.g., cell phone, smart watch, etc.).

Note: Personnel are prohibited from accessing or retrieving data during the game. This will ensure these devices are not being used inappropriately.

Dead-Ball Appeal

When the ball goes out of play all runners must be given an opportunity to complete their base running responsibilities (advancing or returning) as determined by the umpire. The dead-ball appeal cannot be made until the umpire places a new ball into the game and declares "play ball." Once a runner has been given sufficient time to advance or return and shows no immediate intention of doing so, a dead-ball appeal can be made.
See also Rule 7.1.4.

Note: This change provides the defense an opportunity to make a dead-ball appeal, especially on an out-of-the-park walk-off home run, when a runner(s) or the batter-runner misses home plate.

NCAA Rule References
5.3.4, 5.5, 5.9.8, 6.7, 6.12, 7.1.2.2.3, 7.1.4

 **Media Format**

The following media format shall be used in televised games, or may be used by mutual agreement between the two teams or by conference or tournament policy.

Teams are allowed a **maximum of two minutes** between innings and at the start of the game for warm-ups. The following rules are still in effect:

- Warm-up swings on the field of play by the batter who is in foul territory (provided she is outside the batter's box) and the on-deck batter in her team's on-deck circle
- Warm-up running in the foul-territory portion of the outfield
- A base runner(s) who is on base before a pitching change may lead off her respective base(s) during pitching warm-ups

Except that during this time, the **pitcher is allowed to throw any number of warm-up pitches** as she can within the two minutes allowed. She may still only throw to first base once.

The time limit may be shortened by mutual agreement between the two teams or by conference or tournament policy. If a television agreement requires a longer time limit between innings and at the start of the game, that time will become the maximum allowable time.

NCAA Umpire - Media Format Procedure
- The 2 minutes allowed will begin when the last defensive player(s) crosses the foul line closest to their dugout.
- At the end of the 2 minutes, the defensive team must be in position to start including the pitcher in the circle ready to pitch. The lead-off batter needs to be at the plate ready to take the signal from her coach and enter the batter's box ready to bat.
- The time between innings will be kept with a stopwatch by the third base umpire in a 3- person crew. In a 2-person crew, it will be kept by the base umpire.
- The umpires will give each team a warning when there are 30 seconds remaining. In a 3- person crew, the third base umpire gives this warning to the team in the third base dugout and the first base umpire gives this warning to the team in the first base dugout. In a 2- person crew, the base umpire will give the warning to the team in the first base dugout and the home plate umpire will give the warning to the team in the third base dugout.
- The pitcher is allowed an unlimited number of warmup pitches in all games with the 2- minute time limit between innings.

- In the event of undue delay by the team leaving the field, in the sole judgement of the home plate umpire, the team that is to take the field may begin warmups by requesting permission from the home plate umpire. In this case, the 2-minute time limit will still begin when the last defensive player(s) crosses the foul line closest to their dugout.
- This 2-minute time period includes the catcher throwing down to second base and any huddle that the defense wants to have before play is started.
- If the defensive team is not ready to play at the end of the 2 minutes, a ball will be awarded to the batter. If the lead-off batter is not ready to bat, a strike will be assessed to the batter. Either team may use one of its 7 charged conferences to avoid the penalty for not being ready to play.
- If the catcher is the third out of the inning or is on base, another player must be ready to warm up the pitcher while the catcher is getting her equipment on.
- If a coach wants to make substitutions, he/she must do so at the beginning of the 2-minute time between innings so the half-inning can start on schedule. If the coach fails to make a substitution at the correct time, a substitution may not be made until the first batter in the half inning completes her turn at bat.
- If using the media format in a non-televised game, if both teams are ready to play before the end of the 2 minutes, the home plate umpire can start the half inning.
- In a televised game with commercial breaks longer than 2 minutes, the umpires will still give a 30-second warning and the same penalties will apply if teams are not ready to start. • In the event of an injury, a field maintenance situation, or any other special circumstance(s), the umpires may exercise discretion in timing the two minutes.

Projected Substitutions

Any player may be substituted for at any time when the ball is dead. A coach may make substitutes by notifying the plate umpire of the forthcoming changes. Substitutes are not required to enter the game at the time the substitution is reported to the plate umpire. Exception: Projected re-entries are **not** permitted.

This rule change improves the flow of the game by allowing a coach to make projected substitutions. Substitutes will now be reported to the umpire without being required to immediately participate in the game, e.g., allowing a coach to report more than one change in the batting order at the beginning of the inning or re-entering the DP before her next at bat. Projected re-entries, i.e., re-entries reported while the substitute is participating (running, batting, playing defense), will continue not to be allowed.

NCAA Rule References

6.7.1, 6.7.1.1, 6.7.1.2, 8.5.1.1, 8.5.1.3

No Huddle Defense

After an out, the defense is allowed to throw the ball around the infield, but then must throw the ball directly to the pitcher. A team cannot huddle at the pitcher's circle or elsewhere.

EFFECT – The umpire shall
- warn the violator and her coach for the first offense in the game
- For any subsequent offense by any member of the warned team in the same game, a ball is awarded to the batter.

Note: This was utilized as an experimental rule during the 2017 season and improved the flow of the game and pace of play.

Obstruction

Obstruction occurs when a defensive player, not in possession of the ball or in the act of fielding a batted ball, impedes a batter's attempt to make contact with a pitch or impedes the progress of any runner who is legally running bases on a live ball. It can be intentional or unintentional. It is obstruction if a defensive player is blocking the whole base/plate or base path without the ball and/or the runner does not have a clear path to the base/plate.
- Once in possession of the ball, the defensive player can be positioned between the runner and the base/plate.
- Obstruction may be ruled even though there is no physical contact.
- The runner may still be called out if she was clearly beaten by the throw. Meaning, at the time the fielder catches the ball, it could not be reasonably expected for the runner to begin her slide, or the runner is out by such a significant margin that the fielder must wait for her to arrive to apply the tag or until she gives herself up. In past years, coaches taught their players to block the base, catch the ball and make the tag. Now defensive players must catch the ball, block the base and make the tag.
- Obstruction can occur on a force or tag play.
- All references to "in the act of catching" have been deleted.

Notes: To allow a base runner a clear path to the base if the defensive player is receiving a throw and does not have possession of the ball in her glove or hand. Defensive players can no longer cause the runner to alter her path to the base by blocking the base/plate or base path without the ball. Removes the vagueness of "in the act of catching" the ball.

NCAA Rule References
9.1, 9.5.1

Pitcher Taking a Signal

Before starting a pitch, the pitcher must comply with the following:

- Both feet of the pitcher must be on the ground in contact with the pitcher's plate
- Any part of each foot in contact with the ground or pitcher's plate must be completely within the 24-inch length of the pitcher's plate.
- While in this position, the pitcher shall pause for a noticeable stop of at least **two seconds**.

This clarification of a previous interpretation ensures the pitcher has a noticeable stop/pause to allow both the batter and umpire to be ready for the pitch.

Illegal Pitch (Effect)

If the batter does not reach first base safely or if any runner fails to advance at least one base, the coach of the offensive team may choose the result of the play or the standard effect for an illegal pitch, which is that a ball is awarded to the batter.

Note: **Base runners are NOT awarded the next base**. (see below)

If the batter is hit by an illegal pitch not swung at, the batter is awarded first base, and other base runners advance one base, only if forced.

If ball four is an illegal pitch, the batter is awarded first base, and other base runners advance one base, only if forced.

An illegal pitch has no effect on a base runner in softball since they cannot leave the base until the pitch is released. The softball rules committee felt that awarding a ball on the batter and a one-base advance for any runner was an excessive penalty on the pitcher's illegal action.

NCAA Rule References
10.2.1.1, 10.2.2, 10.8 Effect

Legal Position in Batter's Box

At the moment of bat-ball contact, the batter may not contact the pitch when any part of her foot is touching the ground outside the lines of the batter's box.

It is increasingly difficult for plate umpires to assure the delivery of the pitch is legal, track the pitch, be aware of the position of the batter in the batter's box on a hit by pitch and see if the batter has stepped completely outside the box at the point of contact. This rule change ensures slappers do not gain an unfair advantage that other batters do not have by being allowed to contact the ball while outside of the batter's box.

Declared Foul Ball

A legally batted ball that is declared foul cannot be changed regardless of additional information that might be made available to the calling umpire.

Exceptions are dead ball awards:
- out-of-the-park home run
- ground rule double
- hit-by-pitch

A foul ball cannot be changed to a fair ball because the umpires would have to make a judgment as to where the base runner(s) would have advanced. These three exceptions have definitive base awards and therefore do not require the umpire(s) to judge where to place the runner(s). In these three instances, incorrect foul ball calls can be changed to fair/dead ball awards when additional information is made available.

Runner Misses Home Plate

If a runner misses home plate and the fielder misses or makes no attempt to tag the runner, the umpire should make no signal, verbal or nonverbal.

By requiring the umpire to make the safe signal, it could be confusing to the offense and they would have no reason to think they missed home plate. By the umpire making no signal it notifies both the offense and defense that something more needs to occur before a ruling can be made.

NCAA Rule References
11.2.5, 11.15.1, 11.21.4, 11.5.2, 11.5.1, 12.10.12, 7.1.1.2.5.a

Running the Bases

The batter-runner is out when she:

- runs the bases in reverse order
- runs intentionally into the outfield between bases
- runs through first base unnecessarily into the outfield on a walk, dropped third strike or any batted ball either to confuse opponents or to make a travesty of the game.

A runner shall not run bases in reverse order or intentionally run into the outfield between bases either to confuse the fielders or to make a travesty of the game. The rules committee believes this tactic, which involves running out of the traditional base path in order to confuse the defense, does not support the spirit and intent of the rule on the runner's base path and makes a travesty of the game.

Ejected Non-playing Personnel (Effect)

In the case where a non-playing person is ejected they:

- Must leave the playing field, dugout and other team areas and be out of sight and sound.
- Out of sight and sound means unable to view the remainder of the contest and the umpires cannot hear any additional comments.
- Shall not communicate (visually, electronically or verbally) further with the teams or umpires.

Suspended Personnel and Subsequent Violations

Suspended student-athletes shall not be in uniform, shall not be allowed in any team area from the time umpires enter the field until after they leave the field, and shall not perform any team duty while serving a suspension. Exception: Suspended student-athletes may be restricted to the dugout if the suspension is to be served while the team is on the road and no other suitable supervisory options are available.

Suspended coaches and other non-playing personnel shall not communicate with any umpire or be in the playing facility once pregame activities have started until the umpires leave the field of play at the conclusion of the game(s). Any violation of the conditions for the suspended person shall result in the game being forfeited.

NCAA Rule References
12.5.9, 12.10.3, 13.2.1 (Effect), 13.13

Runner / Fielder Collision

When there is a collision between a runner and a fielder who is in clear possession of the ball:

- If the defensive player blocks the base (plate) or baseline, the runner may slide into the base and make contact with the fielder as long as the runner is making a legitimate attempt to reach the base (plate). A legitimate attempt is making contact with the ground before reaching the base or fielder.
- The runner must make an actual attempt to reach the base (plate).
- The runner may not attempt to dislodge the ball from the fielder. Contact above the waist shall be judged by the umpire as an attempt by the runner to dislodge the ball.
- The runner must attempt to avoid a collision if she can reach the base without colliding.
- The runner must be called out if she remains on her feet and deliberately, with great force, crashes into a defensive player holding the ball and waiting to apply a tag.

EFFECT - The ball is dead. The runner is called out for deliberately crashing into a fielder, even if the ball is dislodged. If the runner deliberately crashed into a fielder holding the ball before she was put out and, in the umpire's judgment, it was an attempt to break up an obvious double play, the offender and player being played on shall both be declared out. If the deliberate crash occurs after the runner was called out, the runner closest to home plate will also be declared out. If an obstructed runner deliberately crashes into a fielder holding the ball, the obstruction call will be ignored, and the runner will be called out.

If the act is determined to be flagrant, the offender will be ejected for misconduct under Rule 13 (Behavioral ejection). To prevent a deliberate crash ruling, the runner can slide, jump over the top of the defender holding the ball, go around the defender or return to the previous base touched.

The rules committee continues to have concerns about collisions and is now more in line with NCAA baseball and Major League Baseball. This will ensure the health and safety of our student-athletes and provide clarity for umpires when making difficult obstruction calls.

NCAA Rule References
12.5.9, 12.10.3, 12.13

Certification Mark on Bats

NCAA

Bats shall bear either the permanent ASA 2004 or the new fastpitch USA Softball certification mark <u>and</u> be on the current NCAA Approved Softball Bat List. This list is maintained on the NCAA and the SUP websites indicating compliance with the bat performance standard per the appropriate ASTM testing protocol.

With ASA rebranding to USA Softball, USA Softball will introduce a new bat certification mark for adult and Junior Olympic fastpitch as early as the 2019 season. As a result, bats may either continue to be introduced into the market with the ASA 2004 mark or manufacturers may begin to test and stamp models with the new fastpitch USA Softball certification mark as early as the 2019 season.

Both the ASA 2004 and the new fastpitch USA Softball certification mark will be permitted for NCAA competition to indicate compliance beginning with the 2019 season. In addition to the ASA 2004 or new fastpitch USA Softball certification mark, bats will still be required to also be on the current NCAA Approved Softball Bat List.

Please note, this rules recommendation will not require the purchase of new bats as long as current bats are marked with the ASA 2004 certification mark <u>and</u> are listed on the NCAA Approved Softball Bat List. This rules recommendation is simply adding the new fastpitch USA Softball certification mark as an allowable mark to indicate compliance in addition to the existing ASA 2004 certification mark.

NCAA Rule References

3.3.1.4

Appeals (Types)

When an umpire does NOT make a ruling until REQUESTED by a COACH or PLAYER is considered an appeal play. The various types of appeals include:

Dead Ball Only (VERBAL)
- Used for BATTING OUT of ORDER appeals.

Live (IMPLIED) or Dead Ball (VERBAL)
- MISSING a BASE while advancing or returning.
- LEAVING a base on a CAUGHT FLY-BALL before it is TOUCHED.

Live Ball Only (IMPLIED)
- ATTEMPTING to ADVANCE after making the turn at 1st base (overrunning the base).

Asking for help on a particular ruling is NOT considered an appeal, whether originating from another umpire or coach/player. Live ball appeals can be either VERBAL or IMPLIED. Once the ball is dead VERBAL appeals are the only types of appeals allowed.

Making a Live Ball Appeal (VERBAL or IMPLIED)
- IMPLIED: Appeal by any fielder with the ball touching a base (left too soon/missed)
- IMPLIED: By touching a runner that violated –before returning even if standing on another base.

If in the pitching position, pitchers should step backward to avoid an illegal pitch.

Making a Dead Ball Appeal (VERBAL ONLY)
- Once runners complete advancement and time is granted by the umpire it becomes a dead ball appeal.
- Manager, coach or any defensive player can make a verbal appeal on specific player.
- If the ball was thrown out of play – runners are permitted to complete their base running responsibilities before the umpire may rule on any requested appeal.
- **NFHS:** Pitcher can make verbal appeal while contacting the pitching plate with no illegal pitch penalty.
- **ALL CODES:** A coach or any fielder (USAS - "infielder") may make a dead ball - verbal appeal.

 **Timing of Appeals**

Appeals must be made:

- <u>PRIOR</u> to the next legal or illegal pitch
- or at the end of an inning before all infielders (including the pitcher) leave fair territory (and the catcher vacates her position)
- or on the last play of the game before the umpires leave the field of play

RUNNERS may ADVANCE during a LIVE BALL appeal once pitcher no longer has possession of the ball in the circle (or makes play on runner).

LIVE BALL appeals can even be made after a play is attempted on a runner.

Once TIME is called by the umpire, no runner may advance.

Runners may NOT RETURN to touch a missed base once:
- They reach a base beyond the base missed or left too soon on a dead ball appeal.
- They leave the field of play.
- A following runner has scored.

MORE than ONE appeal may be made on a play, but should not be a guessing game.

Missing HOME PLATE (along with a missed or no-tag) can be appealed by tagging runner (or plate) with the ball.

If the appeal was a FORCED 3rd OUT, then prior runs would NOT score.

 Tag-ups are considered "timing plays" and not "force outs," therefore on any appeal for missing a base/leaving too early, scoring of a run hinges on when the APPEAL occurs - not when the violation occurs.

Rule References
USSSA 9.3 / NFHS 2-1 / USAS RS #1; 7-2d; 8-7i; 8-3g / NCAA 7.1.1

Ball Lodges in Uniform

A ball that becomes accidentally lodged in a **defensive** player's uniform shall **remain live** until the umpire judges the ball is no longer playable. (**NFHS/USAS/ NCAA**)

Other codes do not specifically reference this unique situation.

 If the ball becomes lodged in an offensive player's uniform the ball becomes dead immediately.

However, if a batted ball becomes lodged in a defensive player's uniform, this should **not** be considered a legal catch.

 Although not specifically addressed by rule, deliberately hiding a live ball inside a uniform to deceive base runners may be considered unsportsmanlike conduct and penalized based on the situation.

Rule References
USSSA 3 - Catch.B2 / NFHS 5-1 / USAS 8-4g / NCAA 9.7.2; 9.7.3

Ball Rotation Procedure

ALL CODES

The current **GAME BALL** is typically in play until such time as it goes out of play, blocked, or the umpire deems the ball unsuitable for play from damage.

Situation	NFHS	USSSA	USA Softball	NCAA
If both balls do not get hit into play after the first inning.	Must throw the unused ball to start the bottom half of inning.			No Reference
Pitcher has choice of balls to start subsequent innings.	✓	✓	✓	Choice for Any Inning
Compare TWO balls side-by-side when choosing.	Not Permitted Must use the other ball given to pitcher by umpire.			Must return ball before receiving another.
Pitcher may request a new ball to throw.	No	No	OK to remove if Unplayable	At Any Time
Strict ball rotation procedures during inclement weather conditions.	May not apply based on umpire discretion.			None

NCAA

For all games **12 balls** all with the same specifications and from the same manufacturer are required to be available. (2 New + 10 Good) Pitchers also may request a new ball at any time during the game.

Rule References

USSSA 2007 Clarifications pg. 4 / NFHS Umpire Manual
USAS RS #2 / NCAA 10.12

Bats (Legal / Illegal)

Specifications	NFHS	USSSA	USA Softball	NCAA
General Requirements	All bats must be smooth, straight, un-altered and have a closed barrel end.			
Grip Length	10" min - 15" max		6" min - 15" max	10" min - 15" max
Knobs	Securely fastened by mechanical attachment or welded.			
Required Certification Mark on Bat	ASA Approved 2013 Mark	USSSA BPF 1.20 or Less + USSSA Mark on Taper	USA Softball Approved Marks	Approved Mark (ASA or new USA Softball)
Wooden Bats	Legal			Illegal
Maximum Length	34" Maximum Length			
Maximum Weight	38 ounce Maximum Weight			
Bat List	Not appear on USA Softball Banned List	Not Applicable	Not appear on USA Softball Banned List	Team must provide current list for each game
Material Types	Metal, Composite, Fiberglass and Wood permitted in NFHS, USSSA and USA Softball. NCAA permits wood bats for warm-up only.			
One Piece Rubber Grip and Knob	One Piece is Illegal (2019: Adjustable Knobs are Approved)			Flare / Cone is Illegal
Tacky Substance Endpoint	Must end no further than 15" from end of handle			On Grip Only
Slightly Dented Bats	No Burrs or Dents	No Flat Spots or Dents	No Burrs or Dents	
Warming Devices	Illegal / Altered if found	Approved Models Permitted	Not Approved	Prohibited: Renders Bat Altered

USSSA stipulates the bat shall not have choke up devices, exposed rivets, pins, rough or sharp edges or any form of exterior fastener that would present a hazard. Bats shall be free of rattles and burrs.

NFHS allows the bat taper to be rough but it must be solid. No choke up devices are permitted.

Bats (Legal / Illegal)

Altered Bats

This includes any legal bat that is tampered with by removing or replacing parts, painting, thinning walls, lathing, rolling, heating, cooling, or changing the performance characteristics from the original manufacturer.

Use of Altered or Non-Approved Bat	NFHS	USSSA	USA Softball	NCAA
Effect on Batter if Enters the Box with Bat	If completes at Bat -- Batter is Out and both Batter and Coach are ejected	Called out if detected before next pitch to next batter*	Ejected from Game and Tournament	Out and Ejected
Effect on Runners	Runners return to the position occupied BEFORE bat was used.			
Prior Play / Outs	Any outs occurring prior to the discovery will stand.			
Warning Issued	None permitted or required.			
Player Removal	Ejection	Suspension if bat is sent for testing, pending results.	Ejected from Game / Tournament	Ejected
Coach Removal	Ejected	Ejected if altered or non-approved bat		Ejected*

The use of an **ILLEGAL**, **ALTERED**, or **BAT** that has been **REMOVED** from the game previously, carries various penalties from the batter being declared out to both player and coach removal from the game.

*NCAA Note: The head coach is ejected only when a bat that umpires have declared inappropriate and has been removed from the team's set of allowable bats and is then brought to the plate by the batter.

Rule References
USSSA 2.10.A-D; 8.18.W; 7.14.A; 3.5 / NFHS 1-5; 3-6-1; 7-4-2
USAS 7-4b to i,7-6B / NCAA 3.3

Batter Hits Ball Twice

Situation: Batter Still in Box	NFHS	USSSA	USA Softball	NCAA
Bat hits ball a second time.	Dead Ball - Foul Ball			
Batted ball hits batter.	Dead Ball - Foul Ball			

Situation: Batter Out of Box*	NFHS	USSSA	USA Softball	NCAA
Batted ball hits batter's body in <u>FAIR</u> territory.	Dead Ball - Batter is Declared Out			
Batted ball hits bat while still in batter's hands in <u>FAIR</u> territory.	Dead Ball - Batter is Declared Out			
Batted ball hits batter's body in <u>FOUL</u> territory	Dead Ball - Foul Ball			
Batted ball hits the bat while still in batter's hand in <u>FOUL</u> territory.	Dead Ball - Foul Ball			
A dropped bat hits a batted ball in <u>FAIR</u> territory.	Dead Ball - Batter is Declared Out			
A batted ball rolls into a dropped bat in <u>FAIR</u> territory.	Ball is Live and In-Play (Unless the batter intentionally tried to interfere with the ball)			

*Batter OUT of Box means:
Batter first legally contacted the ball while IN the batter's box
and then was contacted by the ball a second time, OUT of the batter's box.

Rule References
USSSA 7.14.F / NFHS 7-4-13 Exception / USAS 7-6K; RS #24 / NCAA 11.14

Batter Prevents Ball from Entering Strike Zone

If the batter prevents the ball from entering the strike zone by any method other than hitting the ball or a pitched ball hits a batter while the ball is in the strike zone:

- The play is considered a dead-ball strike.
- The ball is dead.
- A strike is given to the batter.

 Runners must return to the original bases occupied at the time of pitch.

 When the batter is hit by a pitch that has not yet reached the front line of the batter's box, assuming she did not swing or attempt to bunt.

- The ball is dead.
- It is declared a no-pitch.

 Intentionally preventing the ball from entering the strike zone and making a travesty of the game can result in either a warning for unsportsmanlike conduct, restriction to the bench, or even ejection based on the umpires judgment.

Rule References
USSSA 7.5B / NFHS 7-2-1h / USAS 7-4L / NCAA 10.10.5, 11.13

Batter Steps Out of the Box

Action	NFHS	USSSA	USA Softball	NCAA
Batter must occupy batter's box:	Within 10 seconds after the umpire directs the batter to assume a position in the batter's box <u>or</u> the pitcher is ready to pitch.			
Failure to occupy the batter's box within time limit:	Ball is Dead. Strike is given to the batter. Batter is declared out if this is the third strike.			
Batter permitted to step out of box between pitches with no timeout requested (or granted):	Permitted but risks being charged with delay.		Must keep one foot in batter's box.	Permitted but risks delay*
Batter Requests Time	At umpires sole discretion to grant timeout request. May deny based on situation. *NCAA umpires instructed to deny request unless unusual circumstances.			

Individual rule sets vary, but generally, if a batter **REQUESTS** time-out and it is **NOT GRANTED** but steps out of the box **ANYWAY**:

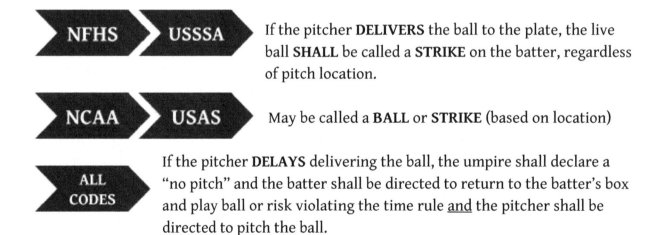

NFHS **USSSA** If the pitcher **DELIVERS** the ball to the plate, the live ball **SHALL** be called a **STRIKE** on the batter, regardless of pitch location.

NCAA **USAS** May be called a **BALL** or **STRIKE** (based on location)

ALL CODES If the pitcher **DELAYS** delivering the ball, the umpire shall declare a "no pitch" and the batter shall be directed to return to the batter's box and play ball or risk violating the time rule <u>and</u> the pitcher shall be directed to pitch the ball.

The **BATTER** shall not deliberately try to **DRAW** an illegal pitch. This act can result in a warning, restriction or ejection. The **UMPIRE** may elect to **GRANT** time-out based on the situation.

Rules Reference
USSSA 7.8 / NFHS 7-3-1 / USAS 7-3B&C / NCAA 10.10

Batter Positioning

The batter is required to **TAKE** a **POSITION** within either of the two batters boxes when directed by the umpire.

Action / Effect	NFHS	USSSA	USA Softball	NCAA
Batter switches batter's boxes after pitcher is in pitching position and ready to pitch.	Ball is dead. Batter is declared out. Runners must return.			Delayed Dead Ball Defensive team may choose the result of the play <u>or</u> batter is out and runners return.
Batter hits fair or foul ball while either foot is touching outside of batter's box <u>or</u> touching home plate.	Dead Ball - Batter is Declared Out if ENTIRE foot is touching ...			Dead Ball - Batter is Declared Out if ANY part of foot is touching ...
Batter intentionally erases a chalk line. (First Offense)	Strike Given to Batter	No Reference	No Reference	Strike Given to Batter
Batter intentionally erases a chalk line. (Second Offense)	Both offender and coach restricted to bench	No Reference	No Reference	Strike Given to Batter

See additional section on "Erasing Chalk Lines" for more information.

Rule References
USSSA 7.4b; 7.10 / NFHS 3-6-17; 7-4-3; 7-4-8 / USAS 7-3d; RS-#7
NCAA 2.8, 11.15, 11.20, 11.21

Batter Struck by Pitch

If a **pitch not swung at strikes the batter,** they are <u>awarded first base</u> without liability to be put out, provided:

 When a batter is hit by a pitch which is **in the strike zone** <u>or</u> if a batter is **swinging at the ball** and is hit by the pitch is shall be considered a dead ball / strike.

<u>No base is awarded</u> – just a strike on the batter.

It doesn't matter if a pitched ball hits the ground before striking the batter – she is still awarded first base.

 The struck batter is awarded first base even if the ball strikes the uniform or clothing, and not her body directly.

Runners advance only if forced.

The batter's hands are <u>not</u> considered to be part of the bat.

If the pitch is within the batter's box, the batter is <u>not required</u> to avoid being hit by the pitch. If the batter <u>obviously tries</u> to be struck by the pitch, the umpire will call either a Dead Ball / Ball <u>or</u> Dead Ball / Strike based on the location of the ball within the strike zone.

 Specifically USSSA and NFHS stipulates that no attempt to avoid being hit by the pitch is required. However, the batter may not obviously try to get hit by the pitch.

 NCAA stipulates the pitch must be entirely within and has reached the front line of the batter's box. Batter struck by pitch outside batter's box and not in strike zone is considered a "dead ball" and a ball is awarded to the batter.

Rule References
USSSA 8.4; 8.4d-note; 10.1/ NFHS 7-3-2, 7-2-1g; 8-1-4b
USAS 7-4h to j; 8-1F / NCAA 11.1

Batter - Runner Overruns First Base

A batter-runner may <u>overrun</u> first base and return directly to it without liability to be put out.

 If she attempts to <u>advance</u> toward second base and decides to <u>return</u> (to first) she is at risk to be tagged out, which is a live ball appeal play

However once the pitcher has control of the live ball <u>within the pitching circle</u> and the Batter-Runner reaches first base the following lookback restrictions may also apply:

- The batter-runner may round first base (towards 2nd base)...
- Stop momentarily...
- Then immediately <u>without stopping</u> again ...

Return to first base **OR** she may advance to second base.

 Provided the batter-runner stops only once <u>momentarily</u> then either <u>advances</u> or <u>returns,</u> it shall be legal. The runner is at liability to be tagged out if the pitcher makes a play on her.

This includes a batter-runner advancing from a walk, dropped 3rd strike, or any legal method while the ball is live. (See Look-Back Restrictions section for more information)

 After overrunning first base and a batter-runner starts moving toward first base and before she touches that base she can go to either first base or second base – provided she stays within the extended base path. Once she makes a move toward <u>either</u> base (steps outside the extended base path) she is committed to that base – either first or second, depending on which way she moved.

Rule References
USSSA 8.2; 8.10; 9.1.D / NFHS 8-7-2; 8-6-8; 8-7-4 / USAS 8-7T(3); RS #37 / NCAA 12.10

Batter-Runner Steps Backward

ALL CODES The ball becomes <u>dead immediately</u> if a batter-runner steps backward toward home plate to <u>avoid</u> (or delay) being <u>tagged</u>.

The batter-runner is declared out.

Other **BASE RUNNERS** must **RETURN** to the last base legally touched at the <u>time of the infraction</u>. (except NCAA)

NCAA Other **BASE RUNNERS** must **RETURN** to the last base legally touched at the <u>time of the pitch</u>.

Regarding USSSA, NFHS and USAS base runners, their location should be noted at the "time of infraction" and not the "time of pitch." If the base runner had legally occupied the next base before the infraction occurred, they should be permitted to stay (or return) to that base. Therefore, if the illegal action of the batter-runner is slow to develop, other base runners may have advanced legally before the infraction occurred.

NCAA rules require runners to return to the last base legally touched at the "time of pitch", which can result in a different effect.

Rule References
USSSA 8.17G / NFHS 5-1-1n, 8-2-5 / USAS 8-2h; RS #33i / NCAA 12.5.7

Batting Out of Order

A <u>proper</u> batter is a player (or substitute) that follows the <u>preceding</u> batter in the lineup. An <u>Improper Batter</u> is considered to be at bat when she enters the batter's box and one pitch is thrown.

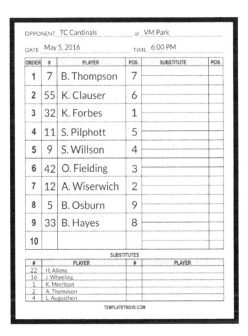

ORDER	#	PLAYER	POS.	SUBSTITUTE	POS.
OPPONENT TC Cardinals				at VM Park	
DATE May 5, 2016				TIME 6:00 PM	
1	7	B. Thompson	7		
2	55	K. Clauser	6		
3	32	K. Forbes	1		
4	11	S. Pilphott	5		
5	9	S. Willson	4		
6	42	O. Fielding	3		
7	12	A. Wiserwich	2		
8	5	B. Osburn	9		
9	33	B. Hayes	8		
10					

SUBSTITUTES			
#	PLAYER	#	PLAYER
22	H. Ailene		
16	J. Wheeling		
1	K. Morrison		
2	A. Thomason		
4	L. Augusthen		

TEMPLATETROVE.COM

Improper Batter

If an Improper Batter is discovered (while at bat), time may be requested, and the batter replaced by the proper batter, assuming the Improper Batter's ball/strike count – as long as this has been discovered <u>before</u> the Improper Batter has been put-out or becomes a base runner.

Only the defensive team can appeal batting out of order, once the batter has completed her time at bat. Batting out of order is an <u>appeal</u> play.

Appeal Procedure

Once the batter completes her at bat:

- It must be appealed prior to the next legal (or illegal) pitch.
- The batter who failed to bat in her proper turn is declared out.
- Umpires should <u>not</u> declare the Improper Batter out. Her time at bat is simply <u>negated</u> and she is returned to the bench.
- All codes (except NCAA): All outs stand and runners must return to their locations at the "time of pitch."
- In NCAA, all outs are nullified.
- Runners advancing by stolen base, wild pitch, passed ball, or illegal pitch are legal.
- Once an Improper Batter reaches base (or is put out) and a next (legal / illegal) pitch is delivered – she is now considered the proper batter.
- Once the defensive team leaves the field after the end of an inning, the Improper Batter is now considered to be the proper batter.
- Once an Improper Batter becomes the proper batter, her actions become legal and stands completely.

Legalized Improper Batter

Once a proper batter is called out because she failed to bat in turn – the next batter shall be the person whose name follows the batter that was called out.

 For NCAA, this is true unless she is on base ... in which case she is skipped and the next batter is the proper batter.

Once an improper batter's actions are legalized, the next batter shall be the person whose name follows the legalized improper batter.

Several Players Batting Out of Order

If several players bat out of order, and it's discovered when a legalized improper batter is on base while it's her turn to bat, she remains on base and is not out.

No runs may score on the play if properly appealed.

 The public-address announcer shall announce the players as listed on the lineup card. The public-address announcer, umpires or official scorer shall not call attention to the improper batter.

If this occurs, the plate umpire shall warn the public-address announcer and/or the official scorer that on the next infraction, he/she will be removed from that position.

Rule References
USSSA 7.2; 9.10 / NFHS 7-1-2 / USAS 7-2a to f
NCAA 11.9 and Appendix B

Blocked Ball - Defined

A blocked ball results when a live batted, pitched, or thrown ball contacts loose equipment or miscellaneous items (not being used legally in the game) in live ball territory.

Additionally when a live ball is touched, stopped, crosses into dead ball territory, or is handled by a person not engaged in the game.

Items Excluded

This <u>EXCLUDES</u> the following items when contacted, as these are <u>NOT</u> to be considered a blocked ball:

- Batters' bat dropped legally
- Catchers' mask removed during play
- Umpires' Equipment
- Players' helmet (accidentally fallen)

Items Included

A blocked ball includes "live ball" touching:

- Or handling by a person not engaged in the game.
- A detached part of a player's uniform, intentionally removed.
- Bats, helmets, or gloves not properly removed from live ball area and placed in dugout appropriately.
- Player's helmet that is removed intentionally while the ball is live and left on the field - (see Helmet Requirements for additional penalties).
- Warm-up equipment not in possession of the on-deck batter.
- When a thrown ball leaves the playing field and lands in dead ball territory.

Blocked Ball - Effect

Team At Bat Causes

Team at bat causes a blocked thrown ball results in an <u>immediate dead ball</u>. (Interference)

 Runner being <u>PLAYED ON is OUT</u> with other runners returning to last base touched prior to blocked ball. If no play is apparent then no runners are out but all runners return.

 Runner <u>CLOSEST to HOME is OUT</u> and other runners return to last base touched prior to blocked ball. If no play is apparent then no runners are out but runners return.

Defense Causes

When the defense causes a blocked thrown ball the ruling is an <u>immediate dead ball</u>. (Interference)

 Overthrown ball rules apply. Runners are awarded <u>two bases</u> from their position (last base legally occupied) at the time of the released throw.

Foul Batted Blocked Ball

Touching loose equipment in foul territory is considered a foul ball.

Team at Bat Blocks Fair Batted Ball

Dead ball and runners advance only if forced based on batter-runner being awarded first base on a hit. If defense was prevented from making a play apply the same effect as thrown ball (above).

Defense Blocks a Fair Batted Ball

Immediate dead ball (Interference). The batter and runner(s) are awarded two based from the time of the pitch.

Rule References

USSSA 3 Blocked Ball / NFHS 2-2-3; 5-5-1g; 8-6-15 / USAS 8-5g (3); RS-#17 / NCAA 9.7 – 9.12

Bunt Attempt

Attempting to legally <u>tap</u> a ball while using any <u>non-swinging movement</u> of the bat should be considered a <u>bunt attempt</u>.

Umpires should focus on the rolling of wrists, bat position / movement, and ball location relative to the strike zone.

Action	NFHS	USSSA	USA Softball	NCAA
Hands / Wrists during the <u>BUNT</u> attempt.	A non-swinging movement with the bat. The wrists are LOCKED as the batter attempts to TAP the ball into play.			
Hands / Wrists during the <u>SLAP HIT</u> attempt.	A swinging movement with the bat. The wrists BREAK during the swinging motion as the batter attempts to STRIKE the ball.			
Holding (Not-Withdrawing) the bat within the strike zone during a bunt attempt	Automatic strike on the batter unless the bat is moving away from the ball.		If bat is not moved toward ball it can be a ball or strike based on the pitch location.	Automatic strike on the batter unless the bat is moving away from the ball
Bunt attempt after two strikes.	If ball is bunted foul the batter is declared out.			
Slap hit attempt after two strikes.	If ball is slapped foul the batter continues with the current count.			

Rule References

USSSA (See 3.Definitions Bunt, Bunt Attempted, Bunt Drag) / NFHS 2-8-1;2-8-3; 2-8-2; 2-9-2
USAS 7-6g & h; RS-#10 / NCAA 11.3.3.5, 11.7.2

Catch Defined

When a fielder **SECURELY GAINS CONTROL** of a batted, pitched, or thrown ball – using her hand(s) and /or glove-mitt, this is ruled a **LEGAL CATCH**.

Legal Catch

First, the fielder must:

- <u>Control</u> the ball.
- The subsequent <u>release</u> of the ball must be voluntary and intentional.
- It's considered a legal catch if the ball is dropped while being <u>transferred</u> to the throwing hand.

Fielders must have possession before going into (or touching) dead ball area. If the fielder catches the ball then falls over (or through) a fence it is still considered to have made a legal catch.

A fielder may contact (or step on) a collapsible fence and still make a catch – provided it is not lying flat*.

No Catch

- Catching with anything other than one's hands or glove in its PROPER PLACE.
- Falling to the ground and not maintaining possession.
- Player uses glove (or uniform) which is displaced from its proper position.
- The defensive players' entire foot is touching dead ball territory - even if part of foot is in the air over live ball territory (ie. toes in the dugout and heel in the air)
- Once a fly ball touches anything other than a defensive player (while in flight) it will be considered a ground ball.
- Trapping the ball against the ground before being caught.

*See Section on "Collapsible Fences" for more details on legal catch vs. no catch situations.

Rule References

USSSA 3 Catch / NFHS 2-9 / USAS 1C; 8-5k / NCAA 9.2

Catch and Carry

Defined
A fielder that <u>unintentionally</u> carries a live ball from playable territory into dead ball territory.

Effect (Unintentional)
A "catch and carry" causes the ball to become dead immediately.

Each base runner is awarded <u>one base</u> from the last base touched at the time of the infraction.

Effect (Intentional)
If in the judgment of the umpire, a fielder <u>intentionally</u> carries a live ball from playable territory into dead ball territory:

- The ball becomes dead immediately.
- Each base runner is awarded <u>two bases</u> from the last base touched at the time of the infraction.

The <u>two base</u> award also applies to a player intentionally pushing, kicking, or throwing a live ball into dead ball territory. The runner's position should also be noted at the time when the infraction occurred.

Rule References
USSSA 10.3I S/B 10.1.I / NFHS 8-4-3 / USAS 1C; 8-5j & k / NCAA 9.4

Catcher Returns Ball to Pitcher

 In all codes, the catcher is required by rule to return the ball <u>directly to the pitcher</u> after each pitch.

Exceptions

These are some <u>exceptions</u> where the catcher may throw the ball to another player, other than the pitcher:

- After a strikeout is made.
- After an actual or attempted put-out is made by the catcher.
- When the catcher is making a play on a base runner.

Effect / Penalty

 1st Offense: When the catcher violates this provision, a <u>ball</u> shall be awarded to the batter.

 In NCAA, the catcher is also <u>warned</u>.
2nd Offense (NCAA only): Catcher is <u>ejected</u> after being warned.

NCAA and USA Softball provide exceptions if <u>any</u> base runners are on. The catcher may throw to any base, <u>even if empty</u>, provided there are other base runners.

 For NFHS, the catcher <u>must</u> be making a play on an actual base runner. Otherwise the penalty would be imposed.

Rule References
USSSA 6.2B / NFHS 6-3-2 / USAS 6-7B / NCAA 10.16, 11.3.2.5

Charged Conferences

A conference is charged (and documented) whenever a coach (or bench personnel) requests and is granted time-out to meet with a defensive or offensive player.

Tracking Conferences

- All conferences should be <u>recorded</u> by the home plate umpire.
- Time out requested for attending to an <u>injured player does not count</u>, provided no coaching occurs while dealing with the injured player.
- The charged conference rule applies once the <u>ball becomes live</u> to start an inning.

Umpires should alert the coach if a timeout is being charged to avoid potential problems later in the game. If excessive timeouts are requested they should be denied by the umpire to prevent additional penalties.

See "Charged Conference - Offense and Defense" tables on following pages.

Rule References

USSSA 4.8 / NFHS 4-7; POE #3 / USAS 5-7; RS #9 / NCAA 6.12

Charged Conference - Offense

Offensive Conferences	NFHS	USSSA	USA Softball	NCAA
Tracking	All conferences are recorded by the Plate Umpire			
Maximum Number	Once ball becomes live -- One Offensive Conference Permitted Per Inning			
Extra Inning Allowance	Teams permitted one additional charged conference per each extra inning			
Requests for Excessive Conference	Umpires should DENY requests for excess conferences beyond the one per inning allowance.			
Excess Results in Additional Penalty	Coach Restricted to Bench			Team Rep(s) or Player(s) who initiate are ejected
Conferring with Base Runners, On-Deck and Current Batter	Coaches are permitted to confer with players and must resume play when directed by the umpire.			
Opposing Team Able to Huddle During Conference	Permitted, provided they are ready to play when umpire is ready to resume play after charged conference.			
When is Opposing Team Also Charged	Opposing team is also charged if they are not ready to play when the umpire directs play to resume.			

Rule References

USSSA 4.8 / NFHS 4-7; POE #3 / USAS 5-7a / NCAA 6.12.5

Charged Conference - Defense

Defensive Conferences	NFHS	USSSA	USA Softball	NCAA
Tracking	All conferences are recorded by the Plate Umpire			
Maximum Number Per Game	Three (3) Permitted Per Regulation Game			One (1) Per Each Inning
Extra Innings	Teams receive one (1) extra conference for each extra inning.			
Excessive Conference Effect	Granting an excess conference results in removal of the pitcher (as a pitcher)			Deny Request
Excessive Conference Removal / Ejection	Coach Restricted to Bench			Team Rep(s) or Player(s) who initiate are ejected
Opposing Team Able to Huddle	Permitted, provided they are ready to play when the umpire directs play to resume.			
No Conference Charged When Changing Pitchers	It is **NOT** a charged conference if the coach talks to a pitcher before removing her as a pitcher.	Same as NCAA	Same as NFHS	It is a **CHARGED** conference if the coach either steps over the foul line or consults with another player **PRIOR** to informing the umpire of the pitching change*
Pitcher Substitutions	Umpire must be notified of pitching changes / substitutions.			

*An additional defensive conference is permitted for each NEW PITCHER entering the game in that half inning. Base runners are not restricted to their bases during warm-up pitches.
Runners are only restricted during suspension of play for the administration of a substitution.

Rule References
USSSA 4.8 / NFHS 3-7-1; 4-7 / USAS 5-7b / NCAA 6.12.4

Checked Swing

To be a **CHECKED SWING** the following observations must be made by the home plate (and base) umpire(s):

- The batter must attempt to **RESTRAIN** the bat from hitting the ball during an attempted hit, slap or bunting.

- The barrel of the **BAT** should **NOT** be carried in front of the batter's body in the direction of the infield.

The plate umpire makes the **INITIAL DETERMINATION** whether the batter **CHECKED** her swing or **STRUCK** completely at the ball.

Once the plate umpire determines the batter **SWUNG** at the ball, this decision in **NOT REVERSIBLE** by a team appealing for help.

If the plate umpire has ruled the batter **CHECKED** her swing, a player or coach **MAY** request the plate umpire for **HELP** from the base umpire, if they are in proper position.

 In **NCAA** contests, the plate umpire **MUST** request help from the appropriate base umpire if requested by the catcher after the pitch is ruled a ball.

The final decision should be based on whether the batter actually **STRUCK** at the **BALL.**

 In games where the two umpire system is used, the base umpire may not be in a good position to assist on "checked swing" calls at the plate. In these cases coaches should realize the plate umpire must bear the burden of determining if the batter swung fully on the pitch

Rule References
USSSA 14.8 Note / NFHS 2-11; 10-1-4N / USAS RS-10 / NCAA 11.10

Collapsible Fences

Facilities that utilize collapsible fences are becoming more popular today. These temporary structures can flex and fold down to prevent injury of a fielder attempting to make a catch.

Here are some guidelines to remember as it relates to a collapsible fence and a legal catch.

- The fielder may **CONTACT** the fence while attempting to make a legal catch.

- The fielder may place **ONE FOOT** (or **BOTH** feet) on the fence which may DISPLACE the fence from a vertical position toward a more horizontal position.

- Contacting the ball (during the catch) while the **FENCE** is **FLEXING** or being displaced is perfectly legal – provided the touching of the ball is **PRIOR** to the fence being **FULLY DISPLACED** or lying **FLAT** on the ground.

- If the fence is **ALREADY LYING FLAT / HORIZONTAL** and the fielder makes contact with the ball, **NO LEGAL CATCH** can be made. In the case of a fly ball -- a home run would be awarded.

USA Softball does not have these same restrictions. A fielder may stand on a fallen portable fence and make a legal catch.

Rule References

USSSA 3.CATCH / NFHS 9-2-7 / USAS Rule Supplement 20; Casebook 1-15
NCAA 9.2.2.2, 9.3.7

Courtesy Runners

All codes (**except NCAA**) **PERMIT** the use of an **OPTIONAL** courtesy runner.

The pitcher or catcher is **NOT** required to leave the game when a courtesy runner is used.

Situation	NFHS	USSSA	USA Softball	NCAA
May use a courtesy runner for pitcher or catcher.	Permitted for either (pitcher / catcher) when she reaches base. This is optional not mandatory.			Not Permitted in NCAA Play
Who is eligible to run?	Any eligible substitute that is NOT in the game can be used as a courtesy runner.			
Last completed at bat (LCAB) can be used if no subs?	Not Permitted	Permitted (New 2018)	Not Permitted	
Not eligible to run.	Once player participates in game.			
Same player may not run for both pitcher **AND** catcher.	Not in Same Game	Not in Same Inning	Not is Same Inning _or_ Game	
Courtesy runner can become a substitute.	Not in same half-inning unless a player is injured and there is no eligible substitutes.			
Courtesy runner permitted for another courtesy runner.	Not Permitted	Only if Injury	Not Permitted	

Continued ...

Courtesy Runners

If a team is using a Designated Player **(DP)** and the **(DP)** is batting only (not playing defense for the pitcher / catcher) they are **NOT** permitted to have a courtesy runner.

Courtesy Runners are not permitted if a **(DP)** or Designated Hitter **(DH)** is batting only and **NOT** playing defense for the pitcher/catcher.

USSSA permits a courtesy runner to become a substitute in the same half inning if injury forces a team to play short-handed. If a courtesy runner is used in the first half inning for the starting pitcher or catcher who does not pitch (or catch) to start the first inning then the player who was a courtesy runner is considered a substitute.

Although Courtesy Runners are **NOT** considered substitutes, they **MUST** be reported to the umpire before entering the game.

Failure for a coach to **REPORT** a courtesy runner carries additional penalties based on the appropriate code:

USSSA: Unreported Substitute Penalty.
NFHS: Unreported Substitute Penalty.
USAS: Illegal Runner (Player DQ'd).
NCAA: Courtesy Runners are <u>NOT</u> permitted at any time.

Rule References
USSSA 8.3 / NFHS 8-9 / USAS 8-10

Double Bases

The following are guidelines for the use of double bases.

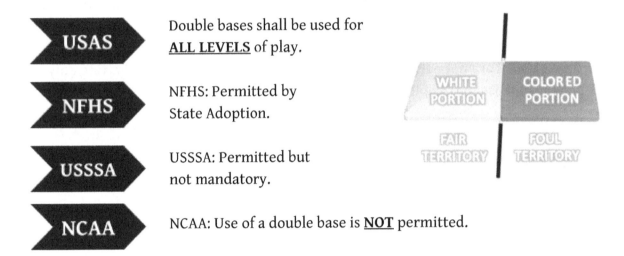

USAS — Double bases shall be used for **ALL LEVELS** of play.

NFHS — NFHS: Permitted by State Adoption.

USSSA — USSSA: Permitted but not mandatory.

NCAA — NCAA: Use of a double base is **NOT** permitted.

- The **DEFENSE MUST** use the **WHITE** portion and the **BATTER-RUNNER MUST** use the **COLORED** portion of the base when a **PLAY** is being made on the batter-runner.
- **Color:** Must be Orange (USSSA) or contrasting for NFHS and USAS.
- The batter-runner can be called **OUT** when a play is being made and they touch the **WHITE** portion **ONLY**. This is considered missing first base and the defense must **APPEAL** before the batter-runner returns to touch **EITHER** portion of the base.
- The batter-runner (or any runner) **MAY USE** the **WHITE** or **COLORED** portion of the base while **ADVANCING** on balls hit to the **OUTFIELD** while no plays are being attempted on the base, while **RETURNING** to first base, while **TAGGING UP** to advance on a fly ball, or returning to the base on an attempted **PICK OFF**.
- The **DEFENSE** may also use **BOTH** portions on these plays or appeals.
- **INTERFERENCE** is called when a collision occurs during a force play and the batter-runner touches **ONLY** the **WHITE** portion of the base.
- **OBSTRUCTION** (Delayed Dead Ball) is ruled when a collision occurs during a force play and the fielder (along with the batter-runner) is touching the **COLORED** portion of the base **ONLY**.
- The **DEFENSE** and the **BATTER-RUNNER** may use **BOTH PORTIONS** of the base on force-out attempts from the foul side of the base, or on errant throws that pull the fielder into foul ground.

Rule References
USSSA 8.19 / NFHS 8-10 / USAS 2-3h; 8-2M / NCAA 2.7

DP / FLEX Guidelines

The Designated Player (DP/FLEX) Rule provides flexibility for athlete participation under NFHS, USSSA USA Softball and NCAA rules.

Overview

By choice **PRIOR** to the start of a game,

- A team may start with nine <u>or</u> ten players as submitted in the official lineup.
- If they start with nine, they can never increase to ten.
- If they start with ten (using the DP), they can, at any time, reduce to nine and/or increase back to ten.
- Under certain circumstances, they may end the game with nine or ten in the lineup.
- The role of the DP is never terminated by rule.

A designated player (DP) may bat for any defensive player (in the field) provided it is made known prior to the start of the game. Once designated to bat for a player, the DP can bat only for that player and any substitutes for that player. The player for whom the DP is hitting (FLEX) must be listed in 10th position of the lineup.

- The DP position, if used, must be indicated in the batting order as one of the nine batting positions.
- Like all starting players, the DP and the FLEX, may reenter the game one time provided it is in their original position in the batting order.
- All players, including the DP and the FLEX, must leave and reenter the game from their original spot in the lineup.
  - *(Note: The FLEX may bat or run in the DP's spot in the batting order.)*
- Substitutes for the DP and the FLEX, must be recorded and tracked in that player's original spot in the lineup similar to any other player.

USSSA utilizes "Additional Players" (AP) as well. AP's must bat and are considered in the lineup, just like the DP. AP's can play defense as well. <u>**If playing for the FLEX -- the FLEX is considered to have left the game, and the lineup is reduced by one**</u>.

About the Designated Player (DP)

- The DP must play offense to be in the game.
- The DP can never play defense only.
- The DP may play defense for any player in the lineup or for the FLEX.

If the **DP plays defense for any player** in the lineup (besides the FLEX):

- That player becomes a batter only.
    - *(NCAA designates this person the Offensive Player or "OP")*
- She continues to bat in her same position in the lineup.
- She has not left the game as the team is still playing with ten.

If the **DP plays defense for the FLEX**:

- The FLEX has left the game.
- The team is now playing with NINE.

 The DP may be replaced as a batter (or runner) by a substitute or by the FLEX. When this situation happens, the DP has left the game and must re-enter (if eligible) in order to be in the game again. If the DP is replaced by a substitute, that substitute becomes the DP and has all the privileges of the DP position. The team is playing with ten players.

If the **DP is replaced by the FLEX**:

- The FLEX is now playing both offense and defense.
- The team is now playing with only NINE players.
- The DP (or the DP's substitute) and the FLEX can never play offense at the same time.

 Index can be found on page 105.

About the FLEX Player

By rule, the **FLEX must play defense** to be considered in the game. Also consider...
The FLEX can never play offense only.

- The FLEX can play any defensive position.
- The FLEX may only play offense for the DP in the DP's position in the lineup.

USSSA: When utilizing the AP, the FLEX may be out of the game defensively, but not considered a substitution.

 If the FLEX plays offense for the DP, the DP has now left the game and the team is playing with nine. Also, the FLEX may be replaced on defense by a substitute or by the DP. When this happens the FLEX has left the game and must re-enter (if eligible) in order to be in the game again.

If the **FLEX is replaced** by a legal substitute:

- That substitute becomes the FLEX and has all the privileges of the FLEX position.
- The team is now playing with TEN players.

If the **FLEX is replaced by the DP** :

- The DP is playing both offense and defense and the team is playing with only NINE players.
- The FLEX and the FLEX's substitute can never play defense at the same time.

 Remember... The **FLEX and the DP can play defense at the same time**. For this to occur the DP must be playing defense for another player in the lineup and not for the FLEX.

Situations Involving the DP / FLEX

If the FLEX is playing offense for the DP and the
DP reenters, or a substitute for the DP enters or
re-enters:

- The FLEX player can return to the
  number 10 position and play defense
  only,
  >Or...
- The FLEX can leave the game if the DP (or
  a substitute) is going to play defense for
  her.

If the DP is playing defense for the FLEX and the
FLEX re-enters, <u>or</u> a substitute for the FLEX
enters or re-enters:

- The DP can remain in the DP position in the lineup and play offense only,
  >Or ...
- The DP can play defense for another player in the lineup,
  >Or...
- The DP can leave the game if the FLEX is going to play offense for her.

Placing the FLEX player into the first nine positions in the lineup for a player <u>other than</u>
the DP is:

- Considered an illegal substitution.
- The illegal substitute (the FLEX) shall be removed (NCAA= ejected) from the game.
- The illegal substitute shall be restricted to the dugout/bench.

Any other infraction involving the DP or the FLEX player is a violation of the substitution rule,
the re-entry rule, or the batting out of order rule.

Rule References
USSSA 3.Designated Player; 3.FLEX, 5.1, 5.3; 5.4
NFHS 2-54, 2-57-1, 3-1-1, 3-3-2, 3-3-6 / USAS 4.3 / NCAA 8.2

Ejections - Where do they go?

PLAYERS after an ejection must comply with the following:

 USA Softball: Must LEAVE the GROUNDS and provide NO CONTACT with umpires or other participants.

 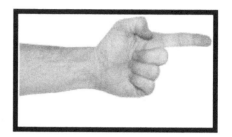 NFHS / USSSA: Players are RESTRICTED to the DUGOUT to maintain proper supervision by coaching staff.

 NCAA: May REMAIN in the DUGOUT but CANNOT COMMUNICATE with opponents or umpires. Subsequent violations shall result in a game forfeit.

NON-PLAYING PERSONNEL after an ejection must comply with the following:

 USSSA/USAS: Must LEAVE the GROUNDS and provide NO CONTACT with umpires or other participants. There is no mention of identifying an alternative head coach to continue the game.

 NFHS: Must LEAVE the VICINITY and is prohibited contact with either team.

 NCAA: The person must leave the playing field, dugout and other team areas and be out of sight and sound. This means they are unable to view the remainder of the contest and the umpires cannot hear any additional comments. They shall not communicate (visually, electronically or verbally) further with the teams or umpires.

NCAA: If the **HEAD COACH** is **EJECTED,** the plate umpire shall ask for identification of the acting head coach replacement. If the head coach refuses to identify the replacement a game forfeit shall be ruled.

Rule References
USSSA 12.1 / NFHS 3-6-20 / USAS 4-8-B / NCAA 13.2

Electronic Equipment

The use of electronic equipment which includes CELL PHONES, RADIOS, iPADS, COMPUTERS, etc... have restrictions on the playing field (and dugout) based on the various rule codes.

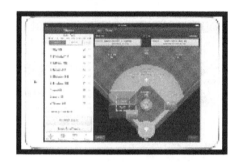

 Cell phones are **not permitted** on the **playing field**. After a warning the offender is ejected if not immediately compliant with the request. Only non-uniformed personnel are permitted to be outside the team areas for purposes of videotaping, recording pitch speeds, running a scoreboard, etc. Team personnel, including players, are prohibited from wearing any device capable of transmitting information while on the field (e.g., cell phone, smart watch, etc.).

Personnel are prohibited from accessing or retrieving data during the game. This will ensure these devices are not being used inappropriately. Both players <u>and</u> non-players become ineligible to participate in the game if they are recording video. For example, if a coach is recording while his team is on defense, they cannot come to the field and coach first base when on offense.

 The use of electronic devices **is permitted** by team personnel in dugout only. However any information obtained shall not be used to review decisions made by the umpires. Parents are permitted to record video and give to the coach but it must be used in the dugout only. No team personnel shall capture video outside of dugout. Media must remain in designated "media / dead ball area."

 Electronic equipment **may not** be used for **coaching** purposes. Wristband (Play Indicators) are considered legal for players and wristbands must be worn properly by batters. Coaches **may** use electronic aids (iPads, laptops, etc) as a scoring device.

 No electronic equipment may be **worn** or **carried** onto the field. After a **warning**, the offending player / coach is ejected.

Rule References
USSSA 2.5; 11.2G / NFHS, 3-6-11 / USAS 4-7-C5 / NCAA 5.9

Erasing Chalk Lines

NFHS
NCAA

Players, coaches, and bench personnel are not permitted to **intentionally** erase chalk lines within the **batter's box** or on the **field of play**.

- A **strike** is given to the batter if the batter or any member of the **offensive team intentionally** erases a line.
- A **ball** is awarded to the batter if the catcher or any member of the **defensive team intentionally** erases a line.

NFHS

NFHS requires after awarding the appropriate ball or strike for erasing a line, the offending team shall be **issued a warning**.
Any subsequent violations will result in the **offender and head coach being restricted to the bench** for the remainder of the game.

NCAA

Subsequent violations by the same team shall result in the **violator's ejection**. Intentionally erasing the pitchers lane line shall also result in a violation.

USA Softball and USSSA
No specific provision regarding the removal of chalk lines.

Rules Reference
NFHS 3-6-17 / NCAA 2.20.3

Equipment Verification and Misuse

For a NFHS and USA Softball games it should be noted that the contest may **not begin** until the **head coach** attends the pre-game conference.

In USSSA, the head coach must be identified and one adult coach must attend the pre-game conference.

NCAA requires one member of the coaching staff to attend the conference and identify the official scorer. Players and/or designated captains may attend but are not required to do so.

During the pre-game conference the following topics are discussed:
- Head coach (or USSSA adult coach attending conference) VERIFIES that all players are equipped properly. (Except NCAA – not necessary)
- For NFHS - verify all player's **equipment is legal** – as requested by the home plate umpire. This responsibility to verify that players are legally equipped rests with the coach and administration of the school. Pre-game equipment inspections of scholastic contests are no longer required.

For NFHS if **illegal equipment is discovered** in the game after the coach has provided their verification it shall be removed or made legal. This also results in **team warning** being issued and the **next offense** will result in the **head coach and offender being restricted to the bench** for the remainder of the game.

Banging of bats in the dugout to generate noise is considered "misuse" of equipment. All codes **prohibit** the misuse of equipment and using it in a way it was not intended to be used. Banging of bats is specifically prohibited and should be considered an unsportsmanlike act by the offending team.
Additionally the **banging of softballs** inside the dugout in a rhythmic pattern should be prohibited for the same reason (In NCAA only when brought to the attention of the umpire).

Rule References
USSSA 4.8D / NFHS 3-5-1; 3-6-1 /USAS Interpretations / NCAA 3.1.2

Forfeit Situations

Failure to Appear on Field

- USSSA / USAS: A forfeit is declared. Refer to Umpire in Chief or Tournament Director.
- NFHS: By state adoption and varies.
- NCAA: This is not a forfeit but rather a "No-Contest" which is declared.

Teams Refuse to Begin / Continue Game

- USSSA: Forfeit after one minute of waiting after warning.
- NFHS: By state adoption. May be a forfeit if team refuses to play or if a team delays greater than 1 minute after the umpire directs the team to "play ball."
- USAS: Forfeit after the proper time as indicated by the tournament association.
- NCAA: Forfeit declared 5 minutes after the umpire has directed teams to "play ball" at the beginning of the game or during the game if one side refuses to play. If after play has been suspended by the umpire one team refuses to play after 2 minutes, a forfeit shall be declared.

Forfeits After Ejections

- USSSA, NFHS, and USAS: Forfeit if order not obeyed within 1 minute of umpires direction. Also if the number of players remaining will be below the required minimum.
- NCAA: Forfeit is not obeyed in a timely manner and a final "60 second" warning is issued and elapsed. Also if the number of players remaining is less than 9.

Who Declares the Forfeit

- USSSA / NFHS: The plate umpire (umpire in chief) has the sole responsibility.
- USAS: Both the plate and base umpires have equal authority.
- NCAA: All umpires must concur in order to declare a forfeit.

Rule References
USSSA 4.7; 14.12N / NFHS 4-3-1; 10-2-2 / USAS 5.4 / NCAA 6.20

Game Limits

Situation	NFHS	USSSA	USA Softball	NCAA
After 5 or more complete innings <u>or</u> 4 ½ with home team ahead.	By State Adoption	8 Runs Ahead	8 Runs Ahead	8 Runs Ahead
After 4 complete innings <u>or</u> 3 ½ with home team ahead.		10 Runs Ahead	12 Runs Ahead	--
After 3 complete innings or 2 ½ with home team ahead.		12 Runs Ahead	15 Runs Ahead	--
International Tiebreaker Rule	By State Adoption	To start 8th inning or after time limit		May be used in 10th inning or determined by conference or tournament policy. Discussed in pregame lineup exchange.
Game can end in a tie.	By State Adoption	Yes, during pool play	Not permitted in tournament play. Resume at POI	Considered regulation game. Leagues may use halted game rule to finish from POI
Who declares forfeit or termination?	Plate Umpire	Tourney Director	Plate or Base Umpire	All Umpires Must Concur
Forfeited / Terminated Score	7-0 in favor of team not at fault.			

 Prudent umpires should continually encourage the two teams' scorekeepers to verify the run count and innings are correct after each full inning.
Additionally the plate (or base) umpire may keep track (separately) of this information as a third checkpoint during the game.

Rules Reference
USSSA 4.4; 4.5; 4.7 / NFHS 4-2-3, 5&6 / USAS 5-9-A1; 5-11; 5-3 / NCAA 6.14-6.21

Glove Requirements

Illegal gloves, when discovered, shall be **removed** immediately from the game by an umpire.

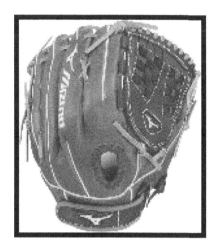

All fielders **must wear a mitt or glove**. The catcher's mitt may be any size. Gloves may not contain tacky or sticky substances.

Colors

NFHS / USAS: Gloves may be a **maximum of two colors** and **lacing is not considered one of the colors**. The umpire may deem any glove's color's to be distracting and request removal.

Gloves that are entirely **optic** (yellow / green) or **color of the ball are illegal** colors and not permissible. Any attachments, printing, designs or optic markings that resemble the appearance of a softball or **deemed distracting** may be considered illegal.

Gloves may be **any color** or combination of colors **except** the color of the ball.

Dimensions

- The **height** of the glove (from heel to highest point) shall **not exceed 14 inches**.
- The **width** of the glove (from the webbing farthest from the thumb to the outside of the little finger) shall **not exceed 8 inches**.
- The webbing shall not exceed 5 ¾ inches. (NCAA shall not exceed 5 inches)

See "Glove - Illegal Use" section (next page) for penalties when detected.

Use of Mitt Style Glove

Any fielder is permitted to utilize a "**mitt**" (first base style or catcher) while **playing any position** if it meets all specifications to be legal.

Rule References
USSSA 2.9 / NFHS 1-4; 8-8-15 / USAS 3-4 / NCAA 3.6

Glove - Illegal Use

NFHS, USSSA and USAS: When a player uses an illegal glove and it is brought to the attention of the umpire a **delayed dead ball** is ruled.

For NCAA, time is called and the glove is removed.

When **no play** is made by the defensive player wearing the illegal glove -- the glove shall be **removed from the game immediately**.

Scenarios

If the player **touched or played a live ball** with the illegal glove and it is detected:

- before the next legal or illegal pitch.
- before the pitcher and all infielders have left fair territory and the catcher has left her position.
- before the umpires have left the field.

The **offended** team's coach has two **options**:

1) The offensive team can **choose** to take the **result of the play** and disregard the illegal act.
2) The offensive coach may choose to **nullify** the entire play with all **runners returning** to original positions at the "time of pitch." The batter shall **bat over** again with the **same ball/strike count** prior to the play.

USSSA: Awards three bases for touching a batted ball, two bases for touching a thrown ball, or four bases if touching prevented ball from going over fence.

Rule References
USSSA 8.14; 10.2.E / NFHS 8-8-15 / USAS 8-8o; RS #23 / NCAA 3.6 (Effect)

Helmet Requirements

All players **must wear an approved protective batting helmet** while at bat, running the bases and while coaching bases.

MEETS NOCSAE STANDARD ®

Helmet Requirements	NFHS	USSSA	USA Softball	NCAA
Face Guard	Required on all batting helmets.			Optional
NOCSAE Seal	Required to be visible.			
Warning Label	Must be visible under helmet's bill or on the shell.			
Catcher's Helmet and Facemask	Must be worn -- and include double flaps.			Required. Double flaps optional.
Intentionally Removing Helmet During Live Ball Play	First Offense: Warn the offending player and coach. Second Offense: Player restricted to bench and coach ejected.		Player is declared out based on umpire discretion.	Player is declared out. Player ejected if fails to replace helmet after directed by umpire.
Defensive Helmets	Non-Glare Only	Optional	Must be team hat color.	Optional, but all same color.

NCAA and NFHS have banned the use of highly reflective (mirror-like) surfaces on helmets.
NFHS requires batter, catcher and defensive player eye shields to be non-reflective and clear.

Rule References
USSSA 2.1, 2.2 / NFHS 1-6-6 & 8; 1-7-1, 1-8-4 / USAS 3-5A,C,& E / NCAA 3.8

Interference Defined

Interference is when the **OFFENSE** illegally **impedes, hiders, or confuses a fielder**. This can be **physically or verbally** and can also involve an umpire, spectator, or even equipment. Contact is not always necessary to have interference.

Effect (NFHS / USAS / USSSA)

(Except NCAA): Interference (unlike obstruction) causes the ball to become **dead immediately** when it occurs.

When a player (batter or runner) causes interference, they are **declared out** and other **runners must return** to bases last legally occupied at the time of the infraction.

If a runner causes the interference the batter is awarded first base.

Effect (NCAA)

Interference by the **batter** causes the umpire to rule a **delayed dead ball**. The defensive team shall choose either the **result of the play** or the **batter is declared out and runners must return** to their last base occupied (at the time of pitch or when the interference occurred) depending on the type of interference. If a runner causes the interference the batter is awarded first base.

See NCAA Rule: 11.20

Malicious contact by a runner on a fielder (with or without the ball – in or out of the baseline) is **always interference**. When interference is caused by a "Retired Runner or Batter" additional penalties are imposed. (See Interference by a Retired Player section)

Rule References
USSSA 3.Interference / NFHS 2-32 / USAS Rule 1 and RS #33 / NCAA 11.18

Interference by the Batter

The **BATTER** (<u>or</u> sometimes runner) is declared **OUT** if the batter actively (or intentionally) hinders/interferes with the catcher (or another fielder) making a play on a base runner.

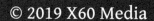

This includes the following situations:

- Batter intentionally interfering with the catcher.
- Interfering by leaning over home plate.
- Hindering a play, throw or action around the home plate area.
- Failure to vacate a crowded plate area.
- Batter interferes with play at the plate with two outs.
  (All Codes: Batter is out, resulting in 3rd out of the inning)
- Batter interferes with play at the plate with less than two outs.
  (NCAA Only: Runner may be declared out - based on choice)

(See previous page for specific penalties and standard effect)

When the batter switches batter's boxes when the pitcher is in position and ready to pitch the batter is called out for disconcerting of the pitcher.**

If the catcher's throw accidently hits the batter or the batter's bat.

- NFHS: Ignore if catcher's throw accidently hits the batter while standing in the box. But if the batter moves and re-establishes position after the catcher controls the ball and is attempting to throw, then this would be considered interference.
- USSSA: Ignored
- USA Softball: Ignored unless the batter is out of the batter's box.
- NCAA: If in the batter's box, ignore. If out of the batter's box this is interference.

**NCAA Reminder: Delayed dead ball is signaled. The defensive team shall choose either the result of the play---- <u>or</u> the batter is out and each base runner must return to the base legally occupied at the time of the pitch or time of interference based on the type of interference.

Rule References
USSSA 3.Interference, 7.12 / NFHS 2-32; 7-4-4a / USAS Rule 1 and RS #33 / NCAA 11.20

Interference by the Batter-Runner

Situation	NFHS	USSSA	USA Softball	NCAA
Running after a dropped 3rd strike. (Entitled to Run)	Interference only if the batter-runner violates the runner's lane provisions			
Running after a dropped 3rd strike. (Not Entitled to Run)	No Interference	Interference and Runner Closest to Home is Declared Out	No Interference	Interference and Runner Closest to Home is Declared Out
Intentionally interfering with a FOUL ground ball.	Interference if umpire judges ball could have been fair.	Not Interference - The ball must be fair.		Interference - batter is declared out.
Running Lane: Throw hits batter-runner with one foot IN and one foot OUT.	If either foot is on ground and outside lane when player is hit - she is declared out.		Depends on area of body hit with ball in reference to lane.	If either foot is on ground and outside either line she is declared out.
Ball hits batter-runner after infield fly situation.	Dead Ball Interference - Runners return and runner closest to home is declared out.		Interference - Runners must return.	Same as NFHS and USSSA

If the batter (not entitled to run to first base) prevents the catcher from attempting a pick-off play by running toward first base in fair territory the runner closest to home will be declared out. Interference must be ruled.

In NCAA play the runner **may** run outside the runner's lane:
- If she has not yet reached the start of the runner's lane
- To avoid a fielder attempting to field a batted ball
- If she leaves the lane on her last stride in order to touch first base

Rule References
USSSA 8.18 / NFHS 8-1, 8-2, 5-1.1e / USAS 8-2 / NCAA 11.20

Interference by the Runner

A **runner** (or batter-runner) that interferes with a fielder executing an initial play causes the ball to become dead immediately.**

Determination must be made whether the interference occurred before **or** after the runner was declared **out** (considered retired) if a play is being made on her.

Conditions for Interference

- Interference occurs if a runner is hit with a **batted ball** before it passes an infielder (other than the pitcher).
- A deflected ball hitting a runner is **not** interference, if **no other player** has an opportunity to make an initial play on the ball.
- Runner must **vacate** (or provide sufficient) space a fielder needs to make a play on a ball – except for the legally occupied base.
- If a runner is off the base and struck by a declared **infield fly**, both the runner and batter are declared out. If two runners are struck by the same fair ball, only the first runner is declared out.

 On a **foul fly ball** that (in the umpire's judgment) could have been caught with ordinary effort, and interference occurs, **both** the **runner** and **batter** are declared **out**. Otherwise, the ball is dead and a strike is awarded to the batter.

 Interference (when called) will automatically cause the ball to become dead immediately. Runners are not permitted to advance after interference is ruled on a runner. NCAA rules stipulate when interference is caused by the batter a delayed dead ball is ruled.

Interference by the Runner

Cause / Effect	NFHS	USSSA	USA Softball	NCAA
Interfering with fielder attempting to field a FAIR FLY ball.	No difference between ground / fly ball. Runner is out and batter awarded first base.		If fielder is prevented from catching ball <u>both</u> runner and batter are declared out.	
Interfering with fielder attempting to field a FOUL FLY ball.	Runner is declared out. Foul ball given to the batter.		Batter and runner are declared out.	Same as NFHS and USSSA
Interfering with fielder attempting to play DEFLECTED ball off other fielder.	Interference if intentional (All Codes) NFHS: Interference if deflects off pitcher and another player has an opportunity to make an initial play.			
Interference on a DOUBLE PLAY attempt.	Succeeding runner is declared out.	Runner closest to home is declared out.	Succeeding runner is declared out	Runner being played on is declared out.

 If a fly ball is hit "into" a **dugout area** and the defender reaches into dead ball area to make a catch, (USSSA, NFHS, and USAS) deem it can be ruled interference, provided an offensive team member actually interferes. However for NCAA, there is no interference if the player is prevented from catching the ball by the player on the bench.

When a fair **batted** ball **touches** a runner who is in **contact with a base,** the following must be considered:

- Runners on a legally occupied base are **not permitted** to **intentionally** hinder a fielder.
- Runners are also **not required** to vacate that base.
- The ball remains **live** if the closest fielder is in **front** of the **base.**
- The ball becomes **dead** if the fielder is behind the base.
- If the ball becomes **dead** the batter-runner is awarded first base and **other runners advance only if forced** by placing the batter at first base.
- In any case, the runner is **not** declared out (while in contact with a base) unless she **intentionally** interferes.

Rule References

USSSA 8.18F,G&H / NFHS 7-4-4, 2-47-3, 8-6-10a / USAS 7-6p; 8-2F3; 8-7 / NCAA 12.17

Interference by a Retired Player

Defined

Interference by a runner after scoring, being called out previously or by a batter after the third strike is **interference** by a **retired player**.

 The word **intentionally** was previously removed from the rule relating to interference by a runner who had been declared out or who had scored. Intent should not be the determining factor in ruling whether interference has occurred by a runner who has scored/been retired.

Effect

If a retired **batter** causes interference:
- The **batter** is **declared out** and...
- The **runner closest to home is declared out** regardless of which runner is being played on.
- Other **runners must return** to the base last legally occupied prior to the interference.

If a retired **runner** prevents a double-play by causing interference:
- The **runner** is already declared out.
- Additionally the **runner** closest to **home** is also declared out.
- The **batter-runner** is awarded first base.
- Other **runners must return** to the base last legally occupied prior to the interference.

 All codes (except NCAA) -- Runners are never permitted to advance after an umpire rules that interference has occurred. The ball becomes dead immediately and runners (not declared out) must return to the base last legally occupied at the time of the interference. The batter-runner is not out because of interference and is awarded first base without liability to be put-out. For NCAA see Interference section for delayed dead ball procedures.

Rule References
USSSA 8.18 H / NFHS 8-2-6, 8-6-18, 5-1-1e / USAS 8-7-P / NCAA 11.20, 12.17.3

Injured Players

If an **injury** of a minor nature occurs during a **live ball** the umpire is directed to wait until:

- The play is complete.
- No further put-out is possible.
- No further advancement is possible.

If the injury appears to be of a **serious nature** <u>or</u> the player is obviously at further **risk** for additional injury, the umpire may:

- **STOP PLAY IMMEDIATELY** to protect an injured player.
- Umpire uses their **judgement** in determining where runners will be placed on the bases, if the ball was to have remained live and play not suspended.

 Umpires and coaches should always err on the side of caution when dealing with injured players. Injured players may return via the re-entry procedure if eligible. (In USSSA, once left the game for injury they may not return!)

A substitute/replacement for an injured **PITCHER** may be given ample time to warm-up prior to restarting the game.

USSSA permits an injured batter / runner to be replaced by the player not currently on base who had the last completed time at bat.

USSSA / NFHS: Athletes that exhibit signs or symptoms consistent with a concussion shall be removed and not permitted to return unless cleared by an appropriate health-care professional. Return procedures also vary by state governing bodies.

Rule References
USSSA 5.9 A / NFHS 3-3-9, 10-2-3g and k / USAS 4-10 / NCAA 15.10.2.3

Jewelry Restrictions

 Stipulate the wearing of **any jewelry** is **prohibited**.

During the pre-game conference, coaches are asked if, "**players** are **properly equipped?**" – including the compliance with no jewelry regulations.

- First offense is a **team warning** and jewelry must be **removed**.
- Second offense results in the offender and head coach **restricted** to the **bench**.

Umpires are directed to remind players that jewelry should be removed before entering the game. Players will not be permitted to participate if directed and fail to remove jewelry.

All Codes: Medical alert bracelets may be visibly worn but must be taped to the body.

 The rule has been modified so as to **allow stud earrings**, while continuing to **prohibit dangling hoops, necklaces, bracelets, rings**, etc judged by the umpire to be **dangerous**. This rule also requires batters to wear play indicators as designed.

NFHS / USSSA: Permit the use of **hair control devices** (even hard items like barrettes, bobby pins, hair clips) provided they are unadorned and no longer than 2 inches in length.

 Requires that exposed jewelry **ruled dangerous** by the umpire must be **removed.**

 Not regulated by umpires.

Rule References
USSSA 2.5; 11.2 D / NFHS 3-2-5, 3-2-12 / USAS 3-6F / NCAA (NR)

Lineup Cards

Requirements on Lineup Card	NFHS	USSSA	USA Softball	NCAA
Starters and available substitutes	Should be accurate - but additional substitutes may be added at any time (Penalty May Apply)			Eligible Subs Not Listed are Illegal Players
Incorrect numbers can be corrected	Penalized if corrected	Correct with no penalty.		Before card becomes official.
DP/FLEX listing	If used must be listed on lineup card to start game.			
AP / EP (Additional or Extra Players) Listed		1 or 2 AP's may be used.	Listed as Extra Players (EP)	
Can add players to lineup during game	Can add with penalty	OK to add eligible players at any time during game.		Considered Illegal Players
First name required	Initial only OK	Full first name required		
Last name required	Full last name required in all codes.			
Uniform Number and Fielding Position	Required by all codes.			
When is lineup official?	After exchanged, verified and accepted by umpire.			Reviewed and submitted to the umpire.
May begin with 8 players?	No	Yes		No
Game forfeited when reach this number of players.	7	7	2 empty batting slots	Anything less than 9
Players in dugout to start game.	Not mentioned	Must be in dugout to start the game		In uniform and dugout.

Rule References
USSSA 5.1 B; 5.3&4 / NFHS 3-1-3 / USAS 1-2; 4-1A; 7-2a to f
NCAA 5.7; 8.3.2, Appendix B

Look-Back Restrictions (Circle Rule)

Look-Back restrictions **apply to all base runners** even though the pitcher is **not** actually "looking" at the runner.

Look-Back restrictions are in effect while:
- The **ball is live**.
- Batter-runner has **reached** first base or has been d**eclared out**.
- The **pitcher has possession** of the ball with **both feet** (completely or partially) within the **pitcher's circle**.

Permissions

Once the restrictions are in effect all runners may **stop once** then must:
- **Immediately return** to that base.

                        or
- **Attempt** to **advance** to the next base.

If the runner is moving when the ball enters the circle, she may immediately stop and go back, but if she keeps moving forward she may not stop.

Effect

Once a **runner stops** at any **base** then **leaves** that base when restrictions are in effect:
- The ball becomes **dead**.
- She is declared **out**.

Exceptions

If the pitcher in control of the ball initiates **action** to cause a **reaction** (of the runner), attempts to **make-a-play** on the runner, or **loses control** of the ball, the runner may choose to:
- Return or advance.
- Is not restricted by the look-back restrictions.

Rule References
USSSA 8.2 / NFHS 8-7 / USAS 8-7t; RS #34 / NCAA 12.16

Obstruction by the Catcher

Obstruction is ruled when the catcher (or another defensive player) **hinders or prevents** the **batter** from **hitting the ball**.

Effect

This is a **delayed dead-ball** play and the umpire will signal appropriately as the play is completed.

Obstruction is **canceled** if the batter:
- Hits the ball and reaches base safely.
- All other runners advance at least one base.
- If so, all action will stand. No additional options are given to the offended team.

.

Otherwise the team at bat **has an option**:

      1) They may **choose** to take the **result of the play**.

             or

      2) Choose the **obstruction penalty** be enforced, resulting with the **batter** being **awarded first base** and the **runners advanced only if forced** by placing the batter on first base.

If obstruction occurs during an attempted **steal of home plate**:
- The batter is **awarded first base**.

             and

- USSSA / NFHS/ USAS: The stealing/squeeze runner is **awarded home** if attempting to advance from third base while other runners advance only if forced.
- NCAA: **All runners advance** whether forced or not.

Rule References
USSSA 8.4. E & Note / NFHS 8-1-1d,e; 8-4-3b / USAS 8-1-D; 8-5B; RS #36
NCAA 9.5

Obstruction by a Fielder

Obstruction occurs when a **fielder** (not in possession of the ball and not making an initial play) **impedes the progress of a runner** (or Batter-Runner) that is legally running the bases. Obstruction can be physical or verbal.

The umpire should utilize the appropriate **delayed-dead ball** signal after obstruction occurs.

Effect

- Runners are protected to the base they would have reached, if there was NO obstruction.
- Runners cannot be called out between the TWO BASES they were obstructed between.
- If the obstructed runner(s) is tagged out, the umpire shall declare a dead ball and award the runner(s) the base(s) they would have reached if there was no obstruction.
- The ball always remains live during obstruction until the umpire declares the ball dead, if necessary.
- If the runner(s) reach their base(s) they would have reached without obstruction, the umpire will drop the delay signal and the ball remains live.

 Runners are **not protected during appeal** if obstructed when returning to touch a missed base, or base left too early on a caught fly ball. Once a runner **obtains** the base they would have reached if no obstruction occurred, and there is a **subsequent play**, they are **no longer protected** if she leaves that base.

In NFHS and USSSA games --fake tags are **always** considered obstruction.
In NCAA and USA Softball - a fake tag must **impede** the runner to be considered obstruction.

Note: In 2018-19 the NCAA has made significant modifications to the "Obstruction Rule." Please refer to the complete breakdown of these changes found in the Rule Change section of this Bluebook edition.

Rule References
USSSA 8.13; 11.2A / NFHS 2-21; 2-36; 8-4-3B / USAS 8-5B / NCAA 9.5

On-Deck Batter / Circle

Requirements	NFHS	USSSA	USA Softball	NCAA
Circle size	5 Foot Diameter / 2 ½ Foot Radius Circle			
Recommended location	30 Feet from Home Plate (Min.)		Safe distance away from Home Plate	
Occupant in circle	Implied to be next batter in circle nearest her dugout.		Must be next batter. Choice of either circle.	Any player nearest her dugout.
Circle may be left empty	Yes		No	Yes
Wear helmet on deck	At all times in live ball area and within the on-deck circle.			
On-deck batter interferes - effect on runners being played on	Runner played on is declared out.	Runner closest to home is declared out. Other runners return to the last base legally occupied at the time of interference.		
On-deck batter interferes with fielder (foul fly ball)	Batter is declared out. Runners must return to last base legally occupied at the time of interference.			
Warm-up attachments	Securely attached items only	No Donuts or Fans. Approved weights permitted	USAS approved devices only	Not permitted in warm-up circle
Max # bats in circle	Total of two bats permitted in circle - maximum. All codes.			
May leave circle	Only for proper turn at bat, provide guidance to advancing runners, or avoid interfering with a fielder making a play.			
Batter's position during pitcher warm-up	Must remain in on-deck circle	--	Must remain in on-deck circle	Must be in foul territory
Warming Devices	Bat is Illegal	Permitted	Bat is Illegal	Alters Bat

Rule References

NFHS 1-1-6; 1-5-1a, 2-5-3 / USAS 3-5E; 3.7; 7-1; RS-16 &33D
USSSA 1.2.J; 2.11; 2.12; 3.On Deck Batter; 3.On Deck Circle; 7.1; 11.2.J / NCAA 11.1

Pitcher's Starting Position

Pitchers may not take the **pitching position** (on or near the pitching plate) without possession of the ball. The pitcher is not considered to be in the pitching position until the catcher is in position and ready to receive the pitch.

Body Position	NFHS	USSSA	USA Softball	NCAA
Pivot foot	To start, must be in contact with the pitcher's plate.			
Non-pivot foot	In contact _or_ behind plate	In contact with pitcher's plate only.		
24" width of plate	Both feet must start and stride foot must finish within the confines of the 24" pitcher's plate. NCAA marks this lane with chalk to start the game.			
Shoulder positioning	Must be in line with first and third base to start	Reference Removed	Must be in line with first and third base to start	No Ref.
Hand positioning	Must start with ball in glove _or_ pitching hand.			
Taking signals	Must pause to take (or simulate taking) signals from catcher or coach on pitching plate			Pause must be 2+ sec.

Hand Movement	NFHS	USSSA	USA Softball	NCAA
Hand start position	Prior to pitch the hands must start apart. NFHS / USSSA: While taking signal. NCAA: During 2 sec. pause.			
Bring hands together in front of body	Not less than 1 sec. or more than 10 sec.	Not more than 10 seconds	Not less than 1 sec. or more than 10 sec.	In view of umpire for not more than 5 sec.
Hands in motion	No Reference	Permitted		
Stepping backward	May step backward anytime	Permitted one step forward and simultaneous with the delivery. Any step backward must begin before the hands come together.		Not permitted.

Rule References

USSSA 6.1 / NFHS 6-1-2; 6-1-1C; 6-4-2 / USAS 6-1; RS #40 / NCAA 10.2; 10.3

Pitcher's Foot Placement

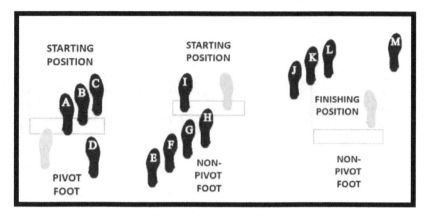

Refer to diagram above.

Foot Placement	NFHS	USSSA	USA Softball	NCAA
Number of feet required on plate	1 or 2 to start	Both feet required to be in contact with the pitcher's plate to start.		
Pivot foot: <u>Legal</u> position to start	A or B is legal. On top or touching the pitcher's plate.			
Pivot foot: <u>Illegal</u> position to start	C and D are illegal. These are not in contact with the plate.			
Non-pivot foot: <u>Legal</u> position to start	F, G, H or I is legal	H or I is considered legal. Must start in contact with pitcher's plate.		
Non-pivot foot: <u>Illegal</u> position to start	E is not legal. Not starting within the 24" width of the pitcher's plate.			
Pivot foot: <u>Legal</u> position to finish	May be in contact with pitcher's plate or drag ground in front of the plate provided there is no loss of contact with the ground or re-planting of the pivot foot.			
Pivot foot: <u>Illegal</u> position to finish	Losing contact with the ground using a hopping motion or re-planting the pivot foot creating a 2nd push point is illegal			
Non-pivot foot: <u>Legal</u> position to finish	K and L are considered legal as they are within the 24" length of the plate to finish			No reference to non-pivot foot. Only stride foot.
Non-pivot foot: <u>Illegal</u> position to finish	J and M are illegal as they finish outside the 24" length of the pitcher's plate to finish			

Rule References

Pitch Starts (When?)

Determining when the pitch actually starts affects the umpire's ruling for an **illegal pitch**.

Once a pitch starts it cannot be discontinued without penalty.

Terminology may be slightly different, but all codes are consistent in the ruling of when the pitch starts.

 Starts when:

- **One hand** is taken off the ball.
         OR
- When the pitcher makes **any kind** of **motion** that is part of the **windup** ... **after the hands** have come together.

 Starts when:

- the **hands separate** ... after the hands have come together.
- The hands may be separated only **one time** per pitch.

Rule References
USSSA 6.1.E.1 / NFHS 6-1-2A / USAS 6-2 / NCAA 10.3

Pitcher Arm Revolutions

During the **delivery** phase of the pitching motion, the following restrictions apply regarding arm revolutions:

Restrictions

- The pitcher may not make more than **1½ clockwise revolutions** in the windmill motion.
- The ball does **not** have to be released the **first time past the hip**.
- After releasing the ball, the arm cannot **rotate past the shoulder**.

- Once the pitcher begins the **clockwise motion** the arm may **not make 2 revolutions**.
- May **not make another revolution** of the pitching motion after releasing the ball.

- Once the pitcher begins the **clockwise motion** that will result in the pitch no more than **1 ½ revolutions**.
- May **not make another revolution** of the pitching motion after releasing the ball.

Effect

Violations result in an **illegal pitch** being ruled.

Rules Reference

USSSA 6.1.G.4&5 / NFHS 6-1-4D / USAS 6-3d / NCAA 10.6

Pitcher Drops the Ball

If the ball **slips** from the pitcher's hand or the pitcher **drops** the ball **during delivery**:

- The batter may still have the opportunity to **strike/swing** at the ball.
- If batter makes a **legitimate attempt** (swinging) at the ball and misses, a strike shall be called.
- Otherwise, it shall be ruled a **ball** on the batter.

Effect

- The ball remains **live**.
- Runners **may advance** with liability to be put out.
- Defensive players **may retrieve the ball** if batter has no opportunity to hit the ball.
- If the batter had a **reasonable opportunity** to hit the ball and the defensive player retrieved it prior, this will be ruled **obstruction**. The ball is declared dead and the batter is awarded first base and all base runners advance if forced. In NCAA, batter and runners are awarded one base whether forced or not.

 Pitchers are not permitted to deliberately drop, roll, or bounce a ball (while in the pitching position) in order to prevent a batter from striking at the pitch. The effect is an Illegal Pitch. If a pitcher drops the ball before the pitch starts, there is no penalty. NCAA stipulates if an illegal pitch occurs but the pitch is not released, it is a dead ball.

Rule References
USSSA 6.1.M / NFHS 6-2-6 /USAS 6-11 / NCAA 10.7

Pitcher / Batter Timing

All codes provide guidelines for both pitcher and batter to keep the flow of a game moving properly. Failure to comply results in a **ball** awarded or a **strike** given to the batter.

Pitcher Requirements	NFHS	USSSA	USA Softball	NCAA
Pitcher must comply after receiving ball from catcher:	Release the pitch within **20 seconds** of receiving the ball.			**10-10-5 sec.** timing provisions**
Failure to comply	A ball is awarded to the batter.			
Batter Requirements	NFHS	USSSA	USA Softball	NCAA
Once ball is returned to pitcher or when directed by the umpire:	Take position in the batter's box within **10 seconds**.			
Failure to comply	A strike is given to the batter.			

NCAA pitchers must comply with the following **timing sequences:

- On **pitcher's plate** within **10 seconds** after receiving ball from catcher or umpire calls, "play ball."
- After batter/pitcher are in position, pitcher has up to another **10 seconds** to bring her **hands together**. During this time must **pause** for a minimum of **2 seconds** to take (or simulate taking) a **signal** from the catcher or coach.
- **After** hands are together the pitcher has up to **5 seconds** to then **deliver** the pitch.
- **Violating** any of these timing sequences results in a **ball awarded to the batter**.

Since a clock is not utilized and umpires are not required to keep visible counts (like other sports) the timing restrictions should be penalized judiciously and used only to prevent unnecessary delays or prevent players from creating an unfair advantage by delaying the game.

Rule References
USSSA 6.1 K; 7.8 / NFHS 6-2-3; 7-3-1 / USAS 6-3o; 7-3b / NCAA 10.18; 11.2

Pitcher - Illegal Pitch Summary

Pitcher Violations	NFHS	USSSA	USA Softball	NCAA
Pitching Plate Violations	Not starting with feet in the proper position in relation to the pitcher's plate. (See Pitcher's Starting Position)			
Pitching Lane Violations	Not finishing with feet within 24" width of pitcher's plate. (Marked as Pitcher's Lane in NCAA contests)			
Taking Signals	Not taking (or simulate) taking a signal properly.			
Bringing Hands Together	Failure to bring hands together or keeping hands together longer than the prescribed limits.			
Taking Position on the Pitcher's Plate	Violation if pitcher takes position on the plate and is not in possession of the ball or takes a position near the plate with ball.			
Remove Herself from Pitching Position	Stepping forward or sideways is illegal. Stepping backward is the only way to legally remove pitcher from pitcher's plate.			
Pivot Foot Violations	Wrong position, leaping, hopping or re-planting pivot foot.			
Deliberately Drop, Roll or Bounce Ball	Violation if batter has no ability to strike at the ball.			
Arm Motion	Excessive or improver revolutions result in a violation.			
Illegal or Distracting Substance on Hand	Based on specific codes -- certain substances are illegal. (See section on Pitching Miscellaneous for info)			
Catcher Violations	**NFHS**	**USSSA**	**USA Softball**	**NCAA**
Not in Proper Position	Not in the catcher's box when the pitcher is ready and in position to pitch or when directed by the umpire.			
Fielder Violations	**NFHS**	**USSSA**	**USA Softball**	**NCAA**
Acts to Distract the Batter	Includes taking a position in line of a batter's vision. Also distracting-unsportsmanlike acts in foul territory.			

For penalties ... see **ILLEGAL PITCH PENALTY** on next page.

Rule References

USSSA 6.1.a through k / NFHS 6-2-1 & 3 / USAS 6-1 through 7 / NCAA 10.8

Pitcher - Illegal Pitch Summary

Not Released to Batter

If the pitch is **not released** or is **released to a base**:

- The umpire should declare an immediate dead ball.
- The batter is awarded a ball.

USAS:
- Runners are directed to advance one base by the umpire.

NFHS / USSSA / NCAA
- **Only a ball is awarded** to the batter. **Runners do not advance** unless forced.

Released to Batter

If the **pitch is released**, the umpire shall signal **delayed dead ball** while verbalizing- "illegal" and ... If the batter does **not hit** the pitch (or **become a base runner**):

- The umpire should then signal **dead ball**.
- The batter is **awarded a ball**.

USAS:
- Runners are directed to advance one base by the umpire.

USSSA/ USAS / NCAA:

Only a ball is awarded to the batter. **Runners do not advance** unless forced.

If the **released pitch is hit by the batter** or the **batter becomes a base runner** the batting team can **choose****:
- To accept the **result** of the batter's **play** on the ball.
- To accept the **penalty** – a ball is awarded to the batter (All Codes) and the runner(s) advance one base (USAS Only).

 Exception: If the batter becomes a base runner and all **other base runners have **advanced at least one base** – then **no option** is given.

Rule References

USSSA 6.1.A- K;6.3 / NFHS 5-1-1p; 6-2-7; 6-1-1d / USAS 6-1 to 5, 7A, and 8 / NCAA 10.8

No Pitch Guidelines

The umpire shall declare the **ball dead immediately** by verbalizing **no pitch** when these situations occur:

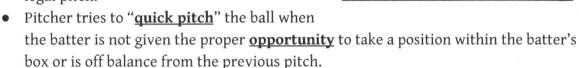

- If the pitcher delivers the ball during the time **play** is **suspended** – when the umpire has declared **time** is **out**.
- The pitch is delivered before the umpire directs the pitcher to **play ball** and makes a **dead ball** – live again or a **batter** steps out of the box causing a **double violation** prior to a legal pitch.
- Pitcher tries to "**quick pitch**" the ball when the batter is not given the proper **opportunity** to take a position within the batter's box or is off balance from the previous pitch.
- After a **foul ball**, the pitcher delivers a pitch to a batter **before** any runners had the opportunity to **retouch** their previously occupied base.
- A coach or player calls **time** for the distinct purpose of causing the pitcher throw an illegal pitch.
- NFHS, USSSA, USAS Only: If a runner **leaves** a base **before** the pitcher **releases** the ball from her hand and is called **out** – the ball is dead immediately and all subsequent action is cancelled. See below for NCAA effect.

A runner leaving early is considered a **Delayed Dead Ball**. At the conclusion of the play the coach of the defensive team shall have the option of:

(1) taking the **result of the play**

or

(2) "**no pitch**" is declared, the batter is returned to the batter's box and the offending runner is out. Base runners must return to the base legally occupied at the time of the pitch.

Rules Reference
USSSA 6.4 / NFHS 6-2-4c / USAS 6-10 / NCAA 10.9; 10.10

Pitching Miscellaneous

Requirement	NFHS	USSSA	USA Softball	NCAA
Warm-up pitches between innings	Maximum of 5 pitches permitted. Additional allowed if replacing an injured pitcher. USSSA additional pitches if umpire finishing duties.			5 pitches permitted**
Warm-up time between innings	Maximum of 1 minute permitted. Additional time if replacing injured pitcher.			Not specified
Unorthodox delivery	Illegal to deliver pitch through legs or behind back			Both legal
Fielders and catchers position	Fielders must be in fair territory and catcher must be in the catcher's box before the pitch is released.			
Wearing distracting items	Pitchers may not wear distracting items on the pitching hand, elbow, forearm or either thigh.			
Taping pitching hand or fingers	Not permitted on contact points	Nothing distracting permitted		Neutral colors permitted
Resin bag or drying agent	Permitted to utilize and leave on the ground in pitcher's circle.			

NCAA ** New for 2018-19: When the optional Media Format is utilized the **pitcher is allowed to throw any number of warm-up pitches** during the allowable warm-up period. She may still only throw to first base once. If not being utilized the standard five pitch warm-up shall be in effect.

 Umpires will typically remind the pitcher/catcher they are not to exceed five pitches between innings – and if they choose to take a warm-up throw down to second base, it should be no later than after the 5th warm-up pitch. Umpires may elect to advise the pitcher/catcher the warm-up period is over if the time limit has been exceeded due to the defensive team being delayed in taking the field to start the inning.

Rules Reference
USSSA 6.1.H&I / NFHS 6-2-2,5&9; 6-1-3C /USAS 6-9; 6-3F; 6-5A; 6-6B / NCAA 10.13, 10.19

Returning to a Missed Base

When a runner **misses a base or leaves too soon**, there are restrictions on how and when the runner must re-touch the base to avoid being called out on appeal.

Ability to Return

Provided the ball remains live and before the defensive team performs an appeal (implied live ball type) the **runner can**:

- Return to a missed base ...
- In reverse order without skipping any bases while returning to touch the missed base.

Too Late to Return

After any of these situations the **runner is not permitted** to return and touch missed bases:

- Standing on a base beyond the base missed **and** the umpire calls time.
- Once the ball becomes dead or time is called.
- Once a following runner has scored (behind them).
- Once the runner leaves the field of play or enters the bench area.
- Once the runner touches the final base of a dead ball award.

Awarded bases must be **touched in order**. When **returning** to touch missed bases they must be **touched in the reverse order** without skipping any bases. Going directly base missed by cutting across the infield is not permitted and the runner may be called out by proper appeal.

Dead Ball Retouch

When a runner is attempting to return (and touch a missed base) and the ball is thrown into dead ball area -- the returning runner should be **given the opportunity** to retouch the missed base(s) or base left early if she is attempting to return.

Rule References

USSSA 8.6.C,H,&K&I; 9.6 / NFHS 8-3; 8-4-3h; 2-1-3a / ASA 8-3G; 8-5G; RS#1D
NCAA 7.1.4; 12.8.3; 12.10.15; 12.10.16

Runner Restrictions

ALL CODES

Runners attempting to advance may legally move **forward and backward** between the bases – **unless**:

- A **play** is being made on the runner.
- Then they must stay within a **three foot base path** (in a straight line) from their **current position** to the base when trying to avoid a **fielder in possession** of the ball.

Batter-Runner Toward First Base

The batter-runner advancing from the batter's box toward first base – is **restricted** from **moving backward to avoid a tag**.

Effect: The Batter-Runner is declared out and runners return to the last base occupied at the time of the infraction (or **NCAA**, the runners base last occupied at the time of pitch).

Hurdling Fielders

Runners **may hurdle or jump** another player provided:
- ASA / NCAA: The runner is trying to avoid a tag and the defender is holding the ball.
- USSSA / NFHS: The **fielder is off their feet** and lying on the ground. However, if the fielder is standing, stooped or crouched the runner may **not leap** over them.

The Standard Effect for this violation is **interference**. The ball becomes dead and runners return to the last base legally occupied at the time of the interference.

Rule References
USSSA 8.18.A and C (Note) / NFHS 8-6-1&10 / USAS 8-8
NCAA 2.6; 12.4.5; 12.10.5; 14.18.3.5

Runners Switching Bases

If runners <u>switch</u> bases after a dead ball or charged conference the following will apply:

Effect	NFHS	USSSA	USA Softball	NCAA
Rule coverage	Covered		Covered	
Effect on runners	Each runner on improper base is declared out	No Reference	Each runner on improper base is declared out	
Offending head coach ejection	If deemed intentional may be ruled unsportsmanlike warranting an ejection.			Head coach ejected
Player removal	Restricted to bench if deliberate			Players involved are ejected
Can be enforced	Not an appeal. Can be enforced by umpire when observed.		Not an appeal. Can be enforced by umpire when observed.	Appeal play after ball is put back into play.

 Intentionally switching players on base during a dead ball is considered unsportsmanlike and should be penalized accordingly. Though not specifically covered in USSSA rules, it may be penalized as such.

Rule References
USSSA 11.2.T / NFHS 8-6-4; 10-2-3f / USAS 8-7Y / NCAA 12.8.3

Spectator Interference

When a spectator reaches into the field of play and **interferes** with a **live ball** the following is in effect:

 The **ball is dead** once a spectator **touches** the live ball in play.

The **umpire** should award the offended team the **proper** compensation (or result) that would have occurred if interference would not have happened.

 If Spectator Interference clearly prevented a fielder from catching a fly ball in the field of play, the ball is dead, the batter is out, and the umpire shall award the appropriate compensation (for example, return base runners to bases, an out, or advance a runner) that, in his or her opinion, would have resulted had interference not taken place.

 If the spectator interfered with a fielder's ability to catch a fly ball, the batter is out and runners are awarded (or returned to) the bases they would have reached if there was no interference.

Rule References
USSSA 8.14.E.1 / NFHS 8-4-3k / USAS 8-2N / NCAA 4.2.1.2, 6.9.4, 12.12.6.2

Strike Zone Defined

There primary difference between the collegiate strike zone and other codes pertains to the "top end" of the zone. NCAA code stipulates a "slightly" smaller zone based on the upper reference point being the sternum versus the armpit. The width remains constant.

[Diagram: Batter's Box dimensions showing 2.18", 3.82", 17", 24.64", 6" measurements]

NFHS / USSSA / USAS

A **strike** shall be called if **any part** of the ball (without touching the ground) passes through:

The **space over home plate** (see diagram -->)

    AND

- **Between** the batter's **forward armpit** and the top of the **knees**.
    - If the batter assumes a **natural** stance.

NCAA

A **strike** shall be called if **any part** of the ball (without touching the ground) passes through:

The **space over home plate** :

    AND

- The **bottom** of the batter's **sternum** to the top of the **knees**.
- If the batter assumes a **natural** batting stance.

The **top** of the ball must be on or within the **horizontal plane**, and either **side** of the ball must be on or within the **vertical plane** of the strike zone to be a strike unless the ball touches the ground before reaching home plate.

When determining the boundaries of a batter's strike zone, the umpire is directed to take notice of the player's "natural stance" within the batter's box. Pitchers should not be penalized for players that crouch down excessively to minimize the strike zone area and intentionally try to draw a walk.

Rule References
USSSA 3.Strike Zone / NFHS 2-56-3 / ASA 1 / NCAA 11.3.1

Substitutions (Legal)

Requirements	NFHS	USSSA	USA Softball	NCAA
Reentry permitted	All starters and substitutes permitted to re-enter one time only.			Starters only one time.
Substitute officially in game when	When reported and ball becomes live.		When reported	When reported, recorded and announced.
Minimum to start game	9 Players	8 Players		9 Players
Minimum number of players to finish	8 players to continue game	Elite Div: 1 less than started with. Other Div's: 8 players min. to continue	8 players	9 players
Effect when reaching absent player	Out is declared.			N/A
If no sub available to replace injured player	Previous batter may replace	**see note		Forfeit
Player arrives late or injured player wishes to return	Late players may be inserted into missing player's lineup spot. Injured players must re-enter into original spot in lineup. USSSA injured player may not return.			Considered illegal if not on lineup
Blood rule	Players leaving game to address blood (on body or uniform) are permitted to return.			Treat without undue delay or penalty

**USSSA Note: Courtesy runner may be used in same ½ inning she was C.R. or she may be replaced by last batter not on base. The injured player may not return.

Rule References
USSSA 5.2; 5.6; 7.14E, 8.3D / NFHS 3-3-3; 3-1-1; 3-3-8; 4-3-1g; 3-3-5
USAS 4-6b; 4-1d; 4-5/ NCAA 8.5

Substitutions (Unreported)

When a player participates in the game without reporting to the umpire the following effects shall be applied.

Effect	NFHS	USSSA	USA Softball	NCAA
How unreported subs are handled	Umpire can take action when noticed or brought to their attention.		By protest.	By appeal.
Player becomes legal in game	After next pitch play stands	After team warning is legal	After next pitch except if batter reaches base	Player is called out then is considered in game
No penalty if violating team				Informs umpire before offended team's challenge
First offense results in (effect):	Head coach warning.	Team warning.	If before next pitch the player is out and runners return.	Depend on timing. Player called out and various effects on resulting play. (See NCAA rules)
Next offense results in (effect):	Offender and head coach restricted to bench.	Coach is ejected.		

Rule References

USSSA 5.5 / NFHS 3-6-7 / USAS 4-6C / NCAA 8.3.3; Appendix B

Substitutions (Illegal)

Defined

A player that enters (or re-enters) the game and does **not have eligibility** or is **not entitled** to enter is considered illegal.

Examples

- Re-entering in the wrong position in the batting order.
- FLEX player violations -- such as entering the lineup in a spot other than the Designated Player (DP) spot
- Courtesy-Runner violations.
- Re-entering the game after being disqualified or ejected.
- Illegal pitchers, batters, or runners.

Player Becomes Illegal When

- NFHS: When ball becomes live and player takes her position (in batter's box, on pitcher's plate, in field, or on base). Illegal Substitutes are referred to as Illegal Players.
- USAS / USSSA: Once entering the game (at bat/position) and one pitch is thrown. Both codes do not consider the wrong tie-breaker runner as illegal.
- NCAA: When the plate umpire records the substitution <u>or</u> she competes in the game. This is handled as an appeal play. Additionally a non-starter/ re-entering player not listed on the line-up card or the wrong tie-breaker runner, is considered an illegal player.

Rule References
USSSA 5.7 / NFHS 3-4 / ASA 4-6 / NCAA 8.3.4; Appendix B

Substitutions (Illegal)

Effect

- Illegal players are **<u>removed</u>** from the game when discovered.
- The delivery of the next pitch **<u>does not legalize an illegal player</u>** – she still is removed.
- Depending on **<u>when this is detected</u>** (in relation to the next pitch to the next batter) determines the specific effect based on various codes.

See chart on the following page for more.

NFHS Applies to NFHS rules when alerted **<u>prior to the next pitch</u>**:

- Can be discovered by either team or umpire once the ball becomes live and the illegal player takes a position in the batter's box, in the field, or replaces player as a substitute or courtesy runner.
- The player is restricted to the bench for the remainder of the game and called out if on offense.
- If offender advances, scored or causes other players to advance/score the play is nullified and runners must return to base occupied at the time of pitch.
- If an illegal defender touches a batted ball or handles a thrown ball that leads to a runner being put-out (or alters play) – additionally the offense may elect to take the results of the play or accept the penalty (nullify play). Umpire may award bases based on their judgment.
- The batter is permitted to bat again with the same count (if batted ball) or pitch is cancelled if a strike (for a thrown ball.)
- Once the next pitch is thrown to the following batter (for either team) the play stands however the illegal player is removed.

<u>Rules Reference</u>

USSSA 5.7 / NFHS 3-4 / ASA 4-6 / NCAA 8.3.4, Appendix B
(See Other Codes on Next Page)

Illegal Substitutions	NFHS	USSSA	USA Softball	NCAA
Offending team corrects own mistake (Offense or Defense)	No penalty if prior to ball becoming live.	Action before a pitch is thrown can be corrected if not appealed.	Player is DQ'd and all play stands.	Offended player is ejected and all play stands.
Defense alerts umpire while offender is at bat	Player is called out and restricted to bench.	Player is called out. Both player and coach are ejected.	Player is DQ'd and all play stands if protested.	Offending player is called out and ejected. Nullify advances on last pitch but other advances are legal.
Defense alerts umpire after at-bat or courtesy runner and prior to next pitch	Player is called out and restricted to bench. Advance is nullified and outs stand.	Player is called out. Both player and coach ejected. Advance is nullified and outs stand.	Player is called out and DQ'd. Nullify advances and outs stand.	
Defense alerts umpire after at-bat or courtesy runner and after next pitch	Player is restricted to bench. All play stands.	Player and coach are ejected. All play stands.	Player is DQ'd. Substitute enters and all play stands.	Offending player is called out and ejected. All advances are legal.
Offensive team alerts umpire, after defensive player makes play and prior to next pitch	Player restricted to bench. Offended team has option of ROP or nullify play and award bases.	Player and coach ejected. Offended team has option of ROP or re-play last pitch.	Player is DQ'd. Offended team has the option of ROP or return to bat with same count. Runners return.	Offensive coach has option nullify play and repeat last pitch or take ROP and offending player ejected.
Offensive team alerts umpire, after defensive player makes play and after next pitch	Player restricted to bench. All play stands.	Player and coach ejected. All play stands.	Player is DQ'd. All play stands.	All play stands and offending player ejected.

   Index can be found on page 105.

NFHS Softball Field Dimensions

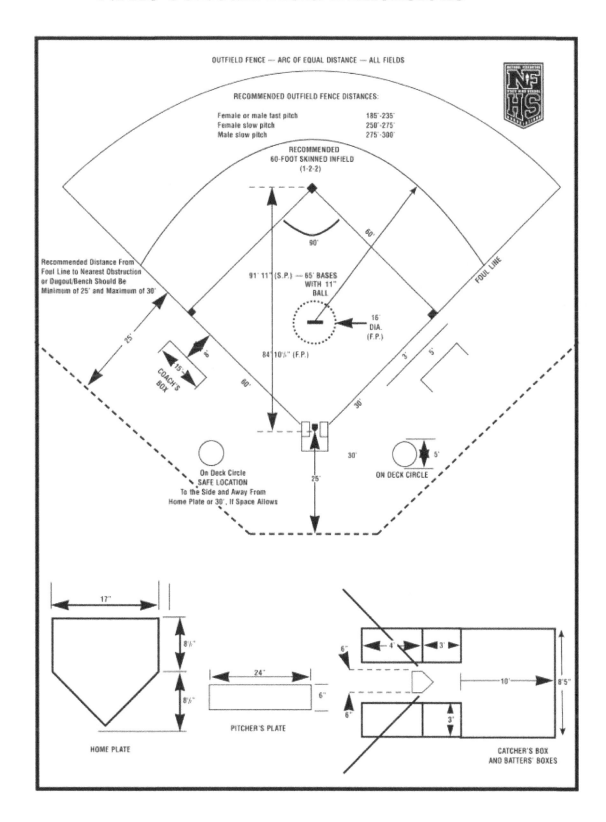

NCAA Protest Checklist

An NCAA protest is a "formal inquiry" into the decision of an umpire and is only permitted (by the NCAA) in the following situations:

- Failure to **apply the correct rule** in a situation.
- Failure to **impose the correct effect** for a given violation of the rules.
- **Misapplication** of a playing **rule**.

They will **not be received** (or considered) if they are based solely on the accuracy of **judgement** of an umpire. Protests may involve matters of both judgement and the misinterpretation of a rule but not judgement solely. The NCAA protest procedure should be carried out by the umpire crew **on the field** using the checklist provided. Cut, fold and laminate this for easy reference in your ball bag. See NCAA Rule 7.2 for more information

NCAA Protest Checklist	Continuing Under Protest
1. Before next pitch (Legal or Illegal)?	12. Plate umpire announces to opposing coach, scorer and PA - game is continuing under protest.
2. Before umpires leave the field?	
3. Umpire decision violates rule? (Not Judgement or Application of Effect)	13. Plate umpire records opponent, date, time, place, crew names, scorer name, rule/section protested, essential facts and contact info.
4. Coach can ID actual rule violated?	
5. Opposing coach may input?	14. If protesting team **wins** then there is "No Protest."
6. Use rulebook in timely fashion?	
7. Crew privately meets / discusses?	15. If protesting team **loses** then plate umpire notifies NCAA Rules Secretary immediately after the game.
8. First attempt to settle?	
9. Bring both coaches together? (Explain ruling - use NCAA Rules Book)	16. Within 24 hours the plate umpire and both coaches file a NCAA Incident Report.
10. Last chance to settle?	**(540) 819-4655**
11. Call NCAA Rules Secretary (for on-field resolution)	Vickie Van Kleeck NCAA Softball Rules Secretary

Index to Rule Topics / Sections

Umpire Pregame Discussion Checklist

(2 Person Umpiring Crews)

Game Situation	
❏ Rule Changes	❏ Run Limit Rules?
❏ Special Game Rules?	❏ Handling Problems / Ejections?
❏ Tie Breaker Inning?	❏ Leaving the Field Post Game
If I could do just ONE THING better this game (compared to last) it would be …	

Basic Crew Responsibilities	
Plate Umpire	**Base Umpire**
❏ All Batted Balls*	❏ All Runners Touch Bases
❏ Fair / Foul - Catch / No Catch	❏ All Plays @ 1st and 2nd
❏ Takes All Plays at the Plate	❏ Take the Initial Play from the Infield @ 3rd Base.
❏ Discuss situations when Plate Umpire covers 3rd Base?	❏ Always take the Batter-Runner to 3rd Base.
❏ Observing Illegal Pitches (Lane / Hands/ Timing)	❏ Observe Illegal Pitches (Feet Only)
❏ Batter-Runner Tag Plays <u>before</u> the start of the runner's lane.	❏ Batter-Runner Tag Play <u>after</u> the start of runner's lane.
❏ Help when BU is started in "C" position? Which plays?	❏ Discuss when to help @ 3rd base with PU is stuck @ Plate.

*Unless Base Umpire chases the play.

Umpire Pregame Discussion Checklist

Fly Ball -- Chase Coverages

Plate Umpire	Base Umpire
❏ Chase All Fly Balls - Move Toward Circle for Credibility	❏ Troubled Fly Ball with Possibility of Trapped Catch
❏ If Base Umpire chases move into see runners touch and take all plays at bases.	❏ Look for Converging Outfielders
	❏ When starting in the "A" Position (on the line) ball hit down the line?
Note: Once BU chases there will be no initial return. PU should be prepared to cover all primary plays. BU can turn and observe and return with clear communication for secondary play or throwbacks. Discuss when?	❏ Ball to CF or RF when starting in the "A" position?
	❏ Chasing the "V" when starting in the "B" or "C" position - not on the line?

Tag-Up Responsibilities

Plate Umpire	Base Umpire
❏ All tags @ 3rd Base	❏ All tags @ 1st Base
❏ **NFHS**: Lead runner with multiple runners on base	❏ **NFHS**: All trail runners tagging. **NCAA**: Takes 1st <u>and</u> 2nd Base
❏ All tags if BU chases	❏ No tag responsibility if chasing.
NCAA: Base Umpire has tagging runner retouching 2nd Base ... Plate Umpire takes tagging runner coming into 3rd Base unless stuck @ Plate	

Umpire Pregame Discussion Checklist

Leaving Base Early

Plate Umpire (None)	Base Umpire (All Bases)
Assist if asked by Base Umpire only. (Primarily @ 2nd Base)	❏ **NFHS / USSSA / USAS**: Immediate Dead Ball - No Pitch
	❏ **NCAA**: Delayed Dead Ball with Options

Crewness Discussion Points

Checked Swing: PU will ask BU for help if needed (or requested). BU will respond with verbal and signal. What is procedure when BU is not on the line?

Pickoff Procedure: Who's call @ 1st Base when the BU is in the "B" or "C" position? Discuss coverage. Always be ready to help IF asked.

Umpire to Umpire Signals: Infield Fly, Dropped 3rd Strike, Two-Out or Timing Play, Request Count or Number of Outs, Special Signals?

Asking for Help: What is our procedure? Missing piece of puzzle?

Confrontations / Ejections: How we will handle these? Fan decorum? Coaches: Discuss play made only. Answer questions only. Partner intervene as needed. Proper escort procedure if needed.

Leaving the Field of Play: Make sure no appeals are apparent. Leave together through agreed upon gate or route. Move directly to changing area.

Discuss Special Situations: Handling the Look-Back Rule, Umpires moving to the next position after the play is over (who moves when?), Run-Downs, Interference / Obstruction and Injured Players

Umpire 5 Minute Postgame Review

1) As a crew, what went **well** today?

2) As a crew (or individual), where did we get **stuck** today?

3) As a crew what should we do **different** next game?

Your Personal Performance Assessment	
Decision Accuracy (Balls / Strikes -- Safes / Outs)	1 - 2 - 3 - 4 - 5
Field Coverage and Mechanics	1 - 2 - 3 - 4 - 5
Game Management	1 - 2 - 3 - 4 - 5
Rules Knowledge	1 - 2 - 3 - 4 - 5
Comportment (Uniform, Demeanor, and Overall Umpiring Presence)	1 - 2 - 3 - 4 - 5

1= Needs Improvement   3= Acceptable   5= Excellent

The **one area** of improvement you will personally focus on for next game is ...

Made in the USA
Columbia, SC
28 April 2019